"I can't seem to put down this book!"

"Dr. Long spoke [at our school] about making a difference in a kid's life. His straightforward, open and friendly approach to sharing simple, yet profound truths with our staff members about at-opportunity children was powerful and moving. I saw many wiping tears as he reminded us all again that a lot of good and effective education requires reaching out to our youth like never before ..."

LAYTON E. WALL — Superintendent, White River Valley
School District, Switz City, Indiana

"This book was great to read as I try to prepare my heart and mind to go back to school. As educators, we all need a pep talk from time to time and your book provided that. Thank you for reminding me of the awesome responsibility I have and the opportunity entrusted to me to guide children. I'm thankful for books like yours that remind me that everything I say and do is watched. It's one that I think anyone who is in direct contact with young people should read. We all need to know how much of an influence we have on them."

ALLISON BOYLL — Teacher

"I can't seem to put down this book! It is easy to read, inspirational, reassuring, and sends such a powerful message ... Thank you for writing this and being so candid, as this will impact many individuals along the way and encourage thinking in a different way and seeing the many angles of children."

ANGIE HALL — Teacher

About the Author

Dr. Long is a lifelong educator and is passionate about helping youth achieve their personal best. This is Dr. Long's third book, his most personal, following *Leadership Tripod* and *They Called Him Joe*. Al also does motivational speaking and conducts various seminars including Power Planning, differentiation, communication, sales and others for public and private organizations. He is a full-time professor at Indiana Wesleyan University where he spends most of his time training leaders. He and his wife Carol founded Power Ventures, Inc., and work each day with their sons Tad, Brad and Chad. Al can be contacted through his website at www.drallong.com.

Other Books by Dr. Al Long

Leadership Tripod

A practical book that applies scientific principles and theories related to learning, decision-making and leadership processes so that executives can retrain their minds to be more effective in dealing with the challenges and emotional dynamics of leadership and organizational change inherent in the business world. Includes such practical tools as pre- and post-knowledge assessments, case scenarios, skills and attitudes toward leadership, plus a leadership interview instrument.

They Called Him Joe

The life experiences of Joe Huff were as varied and colorful as the times he lived through…eras of world wars, the Titanic's demise, man landing on the moon and more. Dr. Long and his son Tad share the inspiring tale of Reverend George "Joe" Huff, an amazing journey of grace and faith as God orchestrates an extraordinary series of events through the life of an ordinary man.

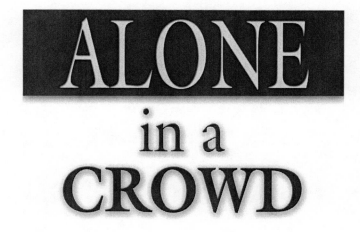

ALONE
in a
CROWD

Brot,
"Always" make
a "difference".

A. Long
2011

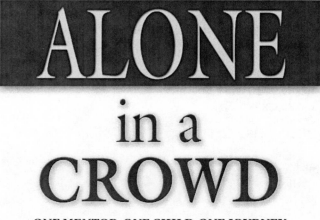

ALONE
in a
CROWD

ONE MENTOR, ONE CHILD, ONE JOURNEY

Dr. Al Long

POWER PUBLISHING
Incorporated

Indianapolis, Indiana

Alone in a Crowd: one mentor, one child, one journey

Dr. Al Long

ISBN-13: 9780978726898
ISBN-10: 0978726898

Library of Congress Control Number: 2007924929

Power Publishing
5641 West 73rd Street
Indianapolis, IN 46278
(317) 347-1051
www.powerpublishinginc.com

This book is manufactured in the United States of America.

Editors: Jennifer Lambert and Janet Schwind
Cover Design: Parada Design

Contents

Acknowledgements
Dr. Al Long

It takes courage and a desire to help others to allow someone to pry as I have pried and prodded to get this book to completion. I would like to thank the members of Lee's family for putting up with me all these years. It would have been easy and understandable for them to have told me to "take a hike," but they didn't, and I am thankful for their understanding. Without their cooperation, this work could never have been completed. My hope and prayer is that through their sacrifice and willingness to share, others will be positively affected.

Finally, I thank my family for their encouragement and positive feedback in pushing me to share with others my journey with Lee. I would like to especially thank you, Coke, my lovely wife, for your support and love through this most emotional trip and for your ideas on how to make the journey even stronger for the reader.

Acknowledgements
Lee

Why anyone had an interest in this "throwaway" kid is not within my understanding, but I do sincerely thank all who have had an impact on my life. To all my teachers and coaches through the years, I just want to say thanks. I would also like to thank my spiritual leaders who mentored me. To all of you who cared about me and my life, I say a heartfelt thanks!

Introduction

It just seems impossible that my family is sitting together at Elliot Hall of Music at Purdue University watching Lee be hooded as he receives his doctorate. This child (now man) who I have watched for so many years is culminating his educational journey not with a period but with an exclamation point. He has just completed his fourth college degree, his Ph.D. This accomplishment is even more special since he came from a home where no one has ever earned even one degree, and some have not even graduated from high school.

A teacher's dream is to be able to make a difference in a child's life and be able to see that child go through life and succeed. That is the feeling we all have while watching Lee walk across the stage, pause in front of the president of Purdue and have the doctoral hood placed over his head. I say "we" because our whole family has been involved in Lee's journey. Lee has really become an extension of ours over the past years, and nearly every major event in his life has been experienced by our entire family. While my frequent meetings with him stopped at the time Lee went off to college to pursue that first degree, our relationship continues today.

This is the story of Lee told from personal taped interviews as well as my own research into this young man's life. In fact, Lee has participated greatly in this book, and when he speaks to you, you will find his words in italics. You will have the opportunity to walk with me as I walked with Lee through his life. My hope is that you will put yourself into Lee's shoes and understand his hope, joy, and sadness, but most especially his desire and ultimate success in finding the keys to unlock the chain of failure in his life.

To unlock the chain, Lee was influenced both positively and negatively by many people. As you read Lee's story, be open to seeing yourself and others around you and learn what I learned from Lee: that we can make a difference. It was said of late President Gerald Ford during his eulogy that "it takes mighty hands to turn the pages of history." It also takes many pairs of hands in a person's life to break the chains of failure. Lee was fortunate enough to have many individuals who showed they cared and got involved in his life. Largely because of them, his life was turned into a success story and the bonds of failure have been broken.

Alone In a Crowd

As a boy I have to say my life was not the best.
I had to survive, but there was little joy and even less laughter.

What I found early in life was I could not be like everyone else.
It took awhile, but I realized I had to be me.

I was hurt so often by those who were supposed to be my friends and care
That I quickly learned to isolate myself...to be alone in a crowd.

1

The Journey Begins

FROM MY FIRST MEETING WITH LEE, he seemed to be "different." Initially, I did not know whether it was a positive or negative difference. He came from a lower class family from a small town in central Indiana. His family had no educational background and struggled with some of the problems many people from that area had: poverty, alcohol abuse, and a general lack of drive for success. But Lee stood out because he just had this incredible drive that could not be missed. As one who wants to have the question of "Why?" answered, Lee quickly instilled overwhelming curiosity in me that I just could not escape. I wanted to watch, learn and see if Lee could succeed and unlock the chain of failure that had seemed to plague those in his family, or if he would do as so many others do and simply follow the path of least resistance.

As an educator I felt I could not go wrong. If he chose to change the pattern of his life, I would know some reasons why; if he chose to stay the typical course of the rest of his family members, I would likewise have some ideas of how to help others. Either way, I could hopefully add to my knowledge to try to understand some of human nature.

The First Meeting

As a member of the staff of a public school, I first met Lee when he came to the junior high school from the local elementary. The teachers from the elementary had sent over his paperwork and had commented how "special" he was. Upon reading his records and looking at his grades, I was intrigued by what "special" meant. I didn't see anything "special" on what they had sent over. I decided I would take the time to find out for myself.

When Lee walked into my classroom, he seemed anything but "special." My first thought was maybe his teachers meant he should be in "special" education. He was a very overweight, plain looking, poorly dressed young boy. He had light, unkempt hair that was evidently longer than it should be. His well worn blue jeans looked at least two sizes too small, and his faded red flannel shirt, also too small, did little to hide the rolls of flesh protruding over his belt. I immediately felt sorry for him. I could imagine that he was probably made fun of by his classmates and was likely a very unhappy child. To my utter surprise, that was not the case at all. Lee seemed to be very well adjusted and cheerful, and he spoke to me as I would expect an adult to, not a poor white kid from a small town.

This first meeting is what sparked my desire to invest my time and emotions in this student. Every meeting I had with him over the next several years just laid credence to that initial meeting. I became more and more intrigued with him and his life. There were so many contradictions in this kid that I just couldn't let him go.

During that first meeting I asked him about his family. I found that he was the youngest of three children. His older brother was eight years his senior, and his sister was four years older. I had not put it together before our meeting, but after this initial discussion I realized I did know of his siblings. I had really not known them well, but did know of the family and I began to understand perhaps what his teachers might have meant when they called Lee "special."

You see, Lee's father was a hard working man, but was well known in the community to drink too much and to gamble when he shouldn't, and he had his family living in one of the worst homes in town. He was a good-hearted man and would do many things for people when he was sober, but when he drank too much, he was what Lee later called a "stupid drunk." He was not mean to his family or others, but he did not show much evidence of success in any area of his life.

Lee didn't know that I knew his family, and in the first conversation we kept our interaction very superficial. I quickly discovered he was a master at covering his real thoughts and emotions. It seemed as though Lee had been through this routine before; he was savvy on how to answer questions and deflect those of a personal nature. Lee was 12, and it was evident he was more in control of himself than his peers. I came away from that first meeting sensing the happiness he seemed to show was masking deeper issues rather than being a sincere emotion. Lee seemed to have already become a survivor at that young age. This simply fueled my interest in his life and what made him tick.

Why the Interest?

I had seen so many children come and go through my classroom that I just couldn't stand to see another possible failure go by without figuring out if I could somehow help. I felt if I could develop a trusting relationship with Lee and his family, I could learn how to more effectively help other students. I had gone through school to be able to help kids, and so far in my short career, I felt I was treading water while children like Lee were drowning around me. If I could just gain some insight of how to help this special young man, maybe other children could be reached. Rather than teaching Lee, I wanted him to teach me about how better to serve the young people I so desperately wanted to help.

All through Lee's middle and high school years we spoke on a regular basis. As he got older, the meetings were a bit sporadic, but I would constantly follow up with his teachers to see how he was progressing. I also spoke to his parents and tried the best I could to find out what was going on at home and how the events could possibly be affecting Lee and his progress in school. It became nearly an obsession to record his thoughts, gain knowledge and delve deep into this young child's journey through life.

2

The First Breakthrough

ALL THROUGH LEE'S middle and most of his high school years, I never felt I was getting the real depth of his thoughts and goals. It was as though he had to hide within himself because he was afraid if he let his emotions out, people would think he was weak or would feel sorry for him, both of which were totally unacceptable to him. In his initial talk with me, though, there was a beacon of light of understanding that shone through his outer wall. That façade of happiness was briefly shattered when, after a few minutes of talking and sharing and Lee finding out that I knew his family, he abruptly changed in demeanor and said in a very forceful manner:

I will not end up like my dad!

I was a bit taken back and really didn't know how to respond. His demeanor changed back quickly to his former self, and it wasn't until much later in our relationship that Lee shared with me that just before our first meeting he had found himself in front of the mirror in his bathroom swearing to be different from his father. It had happened after one of the times when his dad had lost control of his drinking, and it had affected Lee so much that he made a covenant with himself not to end up like his father.

This was really one of the only times through those first few meetings that he let his guard down. It was not until he and I established a mutual trust that he finally came around to telling me his inmost feelings and experiences that had caused this life changing decision. Of course, in the classroom that first day, I had no idea of what direction he had decided to go. Again, however, that is what most intrigued me about this "special" kid.

First Few Years

During the next six years of my relationship with Lee I saw many things that would cause the average observer to believe there was nothing different about Lee. There were times when my wife and family questioned my sanity in my passion to learn about this child. He, for all intents and purposes, seemed to be very much the average or slightly above average kid. As he got older, he lost weight and his grades were always very good. Looking at his report cards and his permanent records, there were only few C's as a sixth, seventh, and eighth grader. From that point on there were no C's and all A's and B's. He became an honor student by the time he graduated sixth overall in his class.

But there was always an underlying sadness about this child juxtaposed with this intense desire to excel. It was evident in everything he did. He first began to play organized sports at a very young age, but since he was overweight, he did not have much success. As he grew older and began to lose some of his weight, he began to have some real victories in the athletic area. As I would have my meetings with him during these early years, he would perk up when I complimented him on his achievements. I didn't learn until much later in our relationship that those compliments were probably all he was receiving.

One of the great things that came from all these years with Lee was that when he finally got older and away from his surroundings, he opened up and shared even more of his innermost thoughts and feelings about his childhood and how he came to learn to survive.

Setting the Stage

The rest of this book will be based on my conversations and meetings with Lee. We continued to meet through his graduation from high school, into his college and post graduate work, and after he had established his family and career. It was only later that he could find the courage to go back in his memory bank and make the withdrawals that will be shared in this book about his life before we met. As stated before, Lee is on board with this and has given his blessing to what is contained in these pages. He has had full editorial rights and has used them many times through this process.

Although our conversations many times jumped from decade to decade and from experience to experience, I have attempted to place his life in chronological order for a better read. I also believe by doing this that you, the reader, will be able to sense the growth, the pain, the joy and the progress of Lee's life up to and through the exclamation point of his life, his doctorate. I hope you enjoy this odyssey as much as I have. As we travel together the life journey of Lee, the boy, to Dr. Lee, the man who still finds himself alone in a crowd, you will see how this really is a story of one mentor, one child, and one journey.

The Early Years

BECAUSE I DIDN'T KNOW LEE before he was 12, I asked him to help fill in this part of his life. To pick up Lee at 12 and not have a glimpse into his past would not allow one to have a full understanding of his triumph.

Lee has shared some times with me when he felt as though he was not much different from everyone else. His earliest memories, however, don't give credibility to what one would consider a "normal" childhood. In a small farming community Lee and his parents lived above a grocery store in a very small town.

I was able to do some research and even found some photographs of Lee's first home. I was also able to talk to some of the people in his home town who still remember what the store looked like and some about the apartment above it.

The store was a small grocery owned by one of the town's wealthier families. They had converted the upstairs storage area into a small apartment. The apartment was accessible only through the back door of the store and then up a flight of very steep stairs. It was well known in the small town that the apartment was not well kept, and the tenants tended to come and go like a revolving door; most of the time it was because of both the shabby conditions of the living quarters and of the tenants' inability to pay the rent.

Listening to Lee and doing some investigating myself, I can't imagine there was a worse place in town for anyone to live. This was just after Lee's dad came home after serving in the Navy, and there was just no other place for them to live. Even having enough food to eat was not always easy. To exemplify this, Lee can share his earliest memory with you.

Because Lee did not feel free to talk about his early life until after he became an adult and our relationship had developed, he is sharing from an adult perspective his memories of his early life. This will give you a glance into why Lee was who he was at our first encounter when he was 12.

I guess it should have given me a clue to how bad my early life was when my fondest and clearest first memory is of food. Looking back from this side of my life, I can see that this was the beginning of my problems with controlling my weight.

My first memory is of a bologna sandwich with mustard. Wow, that is a bit freaky that this sticks so vividly in my mind, but I know it is because we were never starving, but we never seemed to be full. I can still remember how wonderful that sandwich tasted and to this day when I eat bologna, and I do often, I think of the warm feeling that taste and smell gave me. Somehow the sandwich made me think that everything was going to be okay.

Lee's parents had other family members in the area, but the fact that they never took Lee's family in during a time of need speaks volumes as to the lack of family cohesiveness from both Lee's mother's family or his dad's. There was, for whatever reason, no outward expression of concern or compassion for family members who were struggling. Perhaps it was the old frontier spirit, or perhaps it would have been a sign of weakness to admit to needing assistance, but for whatever reason, Lee's family seemed to struggle more than the rest just to try and carve out a meager existence.

The First of Many Moves

THE FIRST HOUSE LEE COULD REMEMBER living in after moving from above the grocery was a run-down rental in a small crossroad village called Max. Of course, this was a step up from where the family had lived before, but in comparison to others it was, as became the norm for Lee's family, one of the worst, if not *the* worst home in the area.

The small village of Max consisted of no more than 20 homes—perhaps 10 on one side of the crudely graded gravel road and 10 on the other. It sat just off a minor state highway. Some of the homes were well kept, but all were older homes. Lee's home was both old and unkempt.

I will try and describe the first house I ever lived in. At the time, I thought it was great! I just remember it was so much larger than where we lived before. It was also out of town in this little crossroads, Max. The house set back off a gravel road and had a lane that ran along the right side. It had no garage, but at least we didn't have to park the old car on the street.

It was like every other house we seemed to live in during my childhood. It had little paint, and what had once been there had long since faded and flaked away. The once white boards on the outside had long since become weathered and a pale grey in color. The front of the house had cement steps going up to a porch. It was the last house before farms started on our side of the road. In fact, the house across the street was a full working farm. The Wrights lived in that house, and they had children who were about the same age as my brother and sister. They all became quick friends, as did the adults. As a matter of fact, those friendships lasted for years after both families moved away from one another.

The interior of the house was very stark and cold, with worn linoleum on the floors and soiled walls. I remember coming in the back door; there was a cellar just to the right of the door, but we did not use it or go down there that I can remember. The house always seemed dark, damp, and cold. That is, cold in the winter, and hot in the summer. There was no central heating or cooling system, and I am sure there was no insulation. My mother would hang plastic over the windows in the winter and put bales of hay around the foundation to keep out the cold and at least slow down the rodents from entering the house.

One of my clearest memories is playing outside one day when it was raining. I remember starting to run up the front steps and slipping on the wet concrete. I hit the corner of my eye on the step and had a rather large gash. Before anyone could get to me, I remember running around the yard crying and blood running down my rain-

streaked face. I was given home first aid. Not taking me to the doctor to get stitches caused me to acquire the scar I still carry on the corner of my eyebrow today. This was the first of a few times when our lack of money prevented a visit to the doctor.

All the life experiences Lee had before I met him had never been shared with any outsiders until now. Listening to his description of this early part of his life was fascinating but also gave me a glimpse inside the child. Again, his seemingly inconsistent reactions were so intriguing. On the one hand, Lee shared the shabby conditions of the home, but on the other hand, you could almost feel the earnestness in his voice when he began to share how excited the family was to move to the "new home."

I know you probably think I'm nuts, but I have such warm memories of moving into that first home and many of the others when we moved. It was something different, and I always thought maybe this would be the time when things would get better. I can remember how hard my mom would work to get the house straightened up and how proud I would be of how it looked. Of course, we still had our old furniture, but in a new surrounding and fairly clean, it always seemed so wonderful.

Yes, maybe I was dreaming and kidding myself, but for those few short hours and days, it was like all was right with the world. It was like we were just like everyone else. It wouldn't take long for something or someone to let me know that was not the case, but man, those moves seemed so great at the time.

When we couldn't move and things would get real

bad, my mom tended to change the placement of the fur-niture. She still does that today. I hadn't really thought about that as I began this trip through my memories , but maybe that is why mom moved the furniture then and still does now — to try to make her feel more in control and better about her life. Maybe that is one reason I tended to move my family so much as I was trying to move my career forward.

Thinking about it now, I can remember seven differ-ent houses or apartments we lived in before I met the Doc, so it's obvious we didn't live in any one place very long at a time. I was so little I had no concept of time, so I really didn't think about the frequency of our moves until now.

5

The First Thread in the Fabric of Lee's Life: People

ISN'T IT INTERESTING that Lee's early childhood events shaped many of his behaviors in his later life? Without giving too much of Lee's story away too quickly, this is the first bit of thread I found in my relationship with Lee: the fact that critical events, but more importantly, people in a young person's life can and do have a huge impact on the overall development of a person. In those words Lee just spoke to you, look beyond what he said about moving and look to what he said when he gave you these words:

> *It was like we were just like everyone else. It wouldn't take long for something or someone to let me know that was not the case...*

As you continue to walk with Lee and me through his life, you will read about times when people do wonderful things for Lee and other times when people say and do things to him that cause great harm. People and how they helped Lee is the first thread.

Stories and Memories of Max, the Village

The Max house was still very early in Lee's life. I continued in our meetings to try to get him to go back as far as he could in his memories and put the pieces of the puzzle of his life together. Lee was still preschool during the Max stay. As he stated before, the move was exciting, but he soon realized all his neighbors and the children he played with had better clothes, the parents had better cars, and food didn't seem to be an issue to others as it was to Lee.

There was a small store at the corner of the road. It was run by a man named Corb Joseph. Although this seemed to be a small part in Lee's development at first glance, as he was telling me of his memories of Max, the interactions with Corb and his store continued to give an insight to Lee's psyche.

I want to tell you about this old store we used to have to go to. As a kid I can remember that I was almost afraid to go in the door. The store was on a curve in Max. It had gas pumps out in front that had long since been useless. The store was totally without paint. It had been that way so long that it was closer to black than grey or white. Not from any paint, but for going so long without any paint, the wood had long since lost its natural color. The store was a simple rectangular building with no signage for the exception of an old metal bread advertisement that served as a door handle on the old screen door on the front. Once in the dirty, dingy structure, there were shelves on either side with no seeming order. In the back of the store was an old meat counter with sliding doors that could only be accessed from behind.

Once at the back of the store and behind the counter,
you could see the area where the owner, Corb, lived. It
was a simple life for a simple crippled man who scared all
of the children of the village of Max.

Lee relates that Corb was bent over at the hip and could not
straighten up. From Lee's description, he resembled the character
in the "Hunchback of Notre Dame." It seems as though Corb
had been a serious drinker in his earlier years, and once, while
bailing hay and being under the influence, he had been struck in
the back of the head with a whiskey bottle and had forever been
disabled.

Lee never really opened up as to why this man was etched in
his memory. While talking, however, my feeling is that this time
was also the first memory Lee had of his father's drinking. One
would wonder if Lee had fear at this tender age that his dad might
end up maimed as well if he didn't stop drinking. To see the devastating effect of alcohol on a man's life had to have affected Lee
at this young, impressionable age.

Corb's small, dirty store also was one of those places that
continually reminded Lee of his poverty. Not many people of
any means ever set foot in the old store. For this reason, most of
Corb's items for sale were outdated, dusty and of little value. The
fact is, however, if you didn't have the money to buy fresh, you
bought what you could afford. Corb's was also the only store in
the area that would accept an IOU for the goods when there was
no money in the house.

When talking to Lee about Corb, he shared that there was
always a rumor that old Corb had money stashed away somewhere in the small store. It served as his home as well as his place
of business, and the small village and area gossip had Corb being

one of the richest guys around, even though you never saw any evidence of his hidden wealth. As I was pouring through the archives of the local paper, I found an old article where someone had evidently believed the rumor and had broken into the store, robbed the old man and, in the process, had hit him in the head with a hammer. Lee remembered the incident and how frightened he and everyone else was that something that evil could happen in their small piece of Middle America.

6

The Unhealthy Thread of Food

LEE'S RECOLLECTIONS ABOUT Corb's store reveal another thread that continues through all of Lee's memory: food.

As I realized from telling you about the bologna sandwich, food was a big deal for me and my family. At Corb's store, all the items were really old. I remember how upset my mom would be when we had to go there and buy anything. If she had to buy any kind of canned goods, when we got them home I could always remember her having to wipe off the dust from the top of the cans. I also remember we got cans that had no labels on them, but Corb had written on each can what was supposed to be contained in the metal container. Sometimes he would be right, but other times we would be surprised as to the contents of the bargain cans of vegetables. We never took them back, however, because they were cheap and we could still make part of a meal from them.

I remember that the thing we bought most from there was probably popcorn. When we could, Mom would buy popcorn for our snack. It's kind of funny that I remember that the popcorn we got from Corb was always in a can. I don't remember seeing popcorn sold that way anywhere else, but it had probably set on his shelves for years before it was ever purchased.

I know the story I am going to tell you will seem silly, but this is how I lived in those years. Although most people could probably have popcorn anytime they wanted it, that was not the case at our home. We rarely had the treat, and when we did, I remember it would be on Sunday nights as we crowded around the television.

Those nights were awesome as I remember, but also awful; awesome because we were as close to a normal family as we could get. Dad would not be drinking because in those days it was illegal to sell any alcoholic beverages on Sunday and he would have consumed everything he had bought before Saturday was over. We would also be together, and we would sometimes have popcorn!

The awful part came because there was never enough to satisfy everyone's hunger for the tasty morsels. On one particular evening I can remember getting a severe spanking because of what I considered just being resourceful. I reasoned that if I could act as though I was eating popcorn and cross my legs just right, I could let kernels fall into my hiding place in my lap that I could skillfully conceal. I pretended to eat ravenously and let morsel after morsel fall between my legs for no one to see. When everyone was done and all were saddened that the entire snack was gone, I cheerfully opened my stash and began to indulge myself on my hidden treasure, to the disdain of my entire family. What I thought should have been totally mine ended up being community popcorn, and I wasn't allowed to be a part of the community. And for my ingenuity I received one of my father's unique spankings. I say "unique" because all through my life I can only remember my father telling me he loved me when he spanked me. He would always preface his punishment by telling me the only reason he was doing it was because he loved me. Many times I wanted to tell him not to love me quite so vigorously, but I never had the courage to ask him to love me a little less.

Food, or a lack thereof, seemed to plague Lee and his family throughout his life. While talking with Lee and taking notes on his responses, I became keenly aware of how some of us may take what we have for granted and not even have a clue of what some children are going through. I thought about my own life—had I ever been so hungry that I had to struggle and scrape for food? Had I ever used food as a salve for the hurting or empty places inside myself? Could I compassionately see past the outward signs of obesity in others to understand the pain that often drives them to seek solace in food?

I also became aware of how food can be a crutch for people by which they limp through the emotions of life. Listening and learning from Lee, it was evident I needed to look beyond the surface of those overweight children or those malnourished looking children and see what was beneath their appearance that perhaps was calling out for help. Maybe if someone in Lee's life could have seen this at an earlier time, he would not have had to go through the pain of being overweight, which he will tell you about later.

At this preschool stage of life, Lee was already beginning to use food as a comfort mechanism. As you can see in Lee's own words, the rare occasions when he ate popcorn were times when he felt normal and safe; that is until he began his hoarding. It is as though the material needs that he didn't have fulfilled and the love he didn't get from his family and extended family could be overcome by the feeling of being full. Not full of love and caring, but full of food. The problem was, and still is for many, the food goes away, but the hurt doesn't.

7

Be Aware and Care

AS PEOPLE WHO SHOULD CARE about the Lees of the world, we need to be aware of those around us who may appear to have eating problems, drinking problems, and drug problems and see if we can find the key to unlock the secrets of the heart and to heal the hurt. People in Lee's life were able to find that key, and it ultimately unlocked the chain of failure in his family.

How many more opportunities to help others have we missed because we have had on the blinders of the world? The blinders stipulate that if people are larger than they should be, skinnier than they should be, don't look right, or don't smell right, they should change themselves. The problem is that a person can't change without someone to help. I used to hear people say, "Those with problems should pull themselves up by their bootstraps." I then heard someone respond, "How can they if they don't have any boots?" It's easy to believe all should help themselves, but they may not have the tools to do so.

Our job as educators, clergy, coaches, and caring human

beings is to tend to those who are less fortunate and help them have an opportunity for a better life. I know that all can't be helped, and there are those few who don't want help, but that can't be used as an excuse for no action.

Lee and many others have found great joy and success because people cared. How many, however, never pull themselves out of their undesirable situations because no one takes the time to throw them a lifeline? I resolved that I would not stand by and do nothing.

The Next Move

As became the pattern through most of Lee's life, there was little stability and moves occurred often. The move from Max came just before Lee started school. The family relocated to a farm just a few miles from Max. It was a move up but the house was still a very old, dilapidated structure located on a working farm. Lee's family did not farm the land, but the landlord, Mr. Slaughter, was a good man and allowed Lee's family to have chickens, pigs and an occasional cow on his land. This did allow for more food as there was also ample space for a large garden. It did not allow, however, for more money coming in or for preventing money going out for alcohol.

It was eye opening to me that Lee continuously spoke of his father's drinking and how that affected him, but also continued to speak of their poverty. This seemed to me to be another of the contradictions of Lee's life. On the one hand, there was no money for food, clothes, and the necessities of life, but on the other hand, there was always money for alcohol. This double standard caused most of the marital problems with Lee's parents and turmoil in his family.

The house we rented from the Slaughter family was far better than the Max house, but looking back it was still one of the worst places around. With no money to buy a home, we had to rent, so in this area we were very limited in where we could live. The house set again on a gravel road that seemed to be fairly heavily traveled. This caused some real problems, especially in the summer. The dust that was kicked up by every passing car caused our house to be impossible to keep clean; not that it would have been anyway. I do remember at one point my dad got some old oil from a gas station somewhere and spread it in front of our house. It helped for a time but quickly soaked into the old road, and the dust went back to its former state.

The house consisted of a living room, kitchen, pantry and two bedrooms downstairs and two bedrooms and a storage room upstairs. It seemed to be huge. Whenever I go by the house now, I am struck by how small it actually is.

It also had a milk house that was attached to the main house by a breezeway. I remember there was no cooling of any kind in this most unique structure, but somehow even in the hottest of the summer months the milk house seemed to be much cooler than anywhere else. There was also a porch that was screened in off the kitchen on the way to the breezeway, and during the summer months this would be used as a refuge from the heat of summer. We would go there to sleep when the house was so hot we could not get any rest.

Siblings Left Alone

It was on this farm that Lee says he remembers for the first time his mother going to work. It may have happened before then, but this was the first time Lee could remember he, his sister, and brother having to stay alone while both their father and mother worked away from home. Although this should have been a good thing for the family as it did allow for more dollars to ultimately come through the door, Lee doesn't have many fond memories of the experience.

I remember when we lived at the Slaughter farm that Mom went to work. She first began to do wall papering for people and she used to take us kids with her. We would help by carrying paper after it was pasted while she climbed a ladder and placed the paper on the wall. This job was not too bad because we got to go with her.

The job was not steady, however, and after I started to school, Mom began working for a local dentist. It would have been okay, but the job she did was to go and clean his house. At that time that is all I needed to feel humiliated. To go to school and be embarrassed for the way I had to dress and to then have to answer the teacher's question of "What do your mom and dad do?" was pretty much devastating to me. As happens many times, the teacher didn't mean anything by her question; she just didn't take the time to think about what it might do to the child who had to answer.

Maybe if she would just have taken the time to notice how I had to bring my lunch to school, she would have had a better idea of how impoverished we were. I can still recall the embarrassment I felt then when I had to carry my lunch on the bus and then on in to school. Most everyone got to buy their lunch, and only the poor kids had to bring their lunch from home. I didn't have a lunch box or anything else to take my lunch in. My mom would take a newspaper and make a square container somehow and that is what I had to carry. Mom wasn't a master of origami; she just didn't have anything else to send the lunch in for me. While any other child who had to bring their lunch seemed to have a cool lunch box—some even with a thermos—I came with my folded newspaper.

Another Thread: Teachers

THIS EXPERIENCE THAT LEE SHARES about his teacher is just the first of many he will be sharing with you, the reader, throughout the book. This is an additional thread that you will see: educators who made a difference. As you read in Lee's acknowledgement, the teachers and coaches in his life were some of the most, if not *the* most, influential people in helping him find the key to unlock the chain of failure. It was impressive to me that when questioned about these teachers, Lee could go through each and every grade of school and name his teacher, his/her characteristics and what made each one special to him.

As could be expected, those early years in school held many sentimental memories for Lee. This "special" boy discovered quickly that education was important, and he longed to succeed from the very beginning. Herein lies an additional seeming contradiction in the life of our subject. You have to understand that this young boy (first or second grade) valued education and wanted to succeed when he was coming from a home where neither his mother nor father graduated from high school, and certainly no one in the family had even the faintest dream of going to college.

The question from the teacher's point of view was "Why?" Why did this child choose to be different? Why did he see value in school when some others coming from the same circumstances didn't? One of the answers can be found in the thread of faculty, the teachers he was blessed to have who took what they did seriously and helped the children under their care to be the best they could be. Lee tells us of his first school experiences:

My first grade teacher was named Mrs. Young, and my second grade teacher was Mrs. Hankins. I don't think there could have been two more different people. Mrs. Young was a kind, loving woman who didn't have a cross word for anyone. She was a very small woman, but her small size didn't hinder her having a huge heart. She cared and loved on all of us, and I can't imagine having a better start to my educational experience.

Mrs. Hankins was mean spirited and seemed at the time not to like children at all. She couldn't have been any more opposite of Mrs. Young in every way. Mrs. Hankins was a very tall woman and, on the surface, had a very small heart of stone. We called her "Hole in the Head Hankins" behind her back because she had a deep impression in the middle of her forehead. This made her look even more intimidating. While Mrs. Young was the matronly role model, Mrs. Hankins was the demanding, stern driver of those in her charge.

As I look back now as a person at the end of my formal schooling, I see I was blessed to have both ladies. I think

Mrs. Young was just what I needed at that time because I was scared, unsure of myself and totally lost being with other children. Mrs. Young made me feel safe and let me know she cared about me.

Mrs. Hankins, on the other hand, scared me to death. I had never been around such a strong woman. Although she came across as mean, she set high standards and would not allow me to fall short. She expected my best and would accept nothing less. She did that for all of her students, but she had a way of making it seem she was focusing only on you and again, that made me feel special. I guess if we could get that point across to anyone who reads this book—that children need to be made to feel special in a good way—then maybe we have accomplished our goal.

Thread of Effective Leaders

The school Lee attended his first two years was an old, run-down elementary school almost in the middle of the small town where he later lived. He then began his third grade year in a brand new K-12 school in the country between two small towns. The first school Lee describes sounds like one that you would see in an old movie. It was two stories with steps running between the floors at each end of the building. The floors were wooden and creaked with the step of each student and seemed to groan under the weight of all the students as they passed from class to class.

During those first two years of formal schooling, Lee developed friendships, work habits, and a desire to learn that would carry him all the way to earning his Ph.D. He shared that during those first formative years he also was made keenly aware of his principal. His first principal at this small elementary was Mr. Fletcher. He was a tall, thin man who was always impeccably dressed. As a matter of fact, Mr. Fletcher was the first man Lee can remember who wore a tie. This was very impressive to Lee. He saw no one in his family or in his circle of influence who ever wore a tie.

Lee remembered how Mr. Fletcher seemed to care about all the children. Mr. Fletcher impacted Lee in a unique way on one occasion that had a life-lasting effect:

One of the most special memories of my early school years was when I was in first and second grade. Our principal, Mr. Fletcher, had a "student of the week" program. Every week a student was picked for this recognition. I can remember thinking if I could just win that sometime, I would be more like everyone else and it would show them that I was just as good as they were. The prize was a candy cane. I can still picture to this day what it looked like and how big it was. For my childlike eyes it seemed to be gigantic, and I just dreamed of how it would taste and how long I could make it last. But alas, I went all the way through the first grade without being named.

Then it happened! I was summoned to the principal's office, and with great fanfare and celebration I was named student of the week. I could barely contain my joy and pride. I was handed the giant candy cane, and I could not have been any more happy or proud than I was then. Someone was probably receiving the Nobel Prize, but I was receiving the giant candy cane. How dare anyone even compare them? Mine certainly was more important, or at least that is what I thought, and the feeling of pride for my accomplishment could not be matched at that point in my life.

The leader of this small rural elementary school cared about those he served. In an earlier book, *Leadership Tripod,* I talked about being a shepherd leader and knowing one's sheep, and Mr. Fletcher exemplifies that type of leader. By performing a small act of kindness for a young child who needed it more than most even realized, he was an integral part in setting Lee on the path of success. He had taken the time and effort needed to recognize Lee's needs and to make sure he was set apart by this small token of success, probably the first affirmation Lee had ever received for doing anything.

As a longtime educator and leader myself, it strikes home to me that I did not always do what Mr. Fletcher did. It breaks my heart to realize the missed opportunities, the chances to build someone up that I may have let go by. Likewise, I see most public and private schools and their leaders have done away with any kind of special recognition for children. The premise is that children who don't get chosen might somehow feel less significant than others. But shouldn't we focus on those we can help rather than those we might miss? The idea that we shouldn't do something because of the "what ifs" is not reason enough to stop forging ahead in trying to acknowledge children in a special way. Listening to how this trivial act meant so much to this small child makes me want to shout to all leaders to start or further develop programs of recognition in their schools. Should we not spend an equal amount of time and energy on rewarding good as we do in punishing bad, and shouldn't we seek ways we can actively help those children who are in need of help?

9

The Faith Thread

IT WAS ABOUT THIS SAME TIME that another inter-loper came into Lee's life to begin his walk toward what I discovered was another thread in his life: faith. Lee and his sister were invited by a neighbor to ride with them and go to their church. No one in Lee's immediate family and neither of his grandparents attended church at this time. To have someone ask was startling, but even more startling was Lee's parents allowing him and his sister to go. Of course, Lee's parents didn't go, but they did permit the neighbor to take their children.

It would make a great story to say this first experience was wonderful, that Lee accepted Christ and lived happily ever after, but it was not to be the case. In fact, after this experience, it is a wonder he ever went back to church. The first adventure evidently went okay, but the second and last trip to this church was permanently tainted by a person who did not understand how words can adversely affect a child. The hurt and embarrassment Lee felt at his second visit took years to overcome.

As everyone who knows me understands, my faith is a huge part of my life as well as my family's. My first experience with church, however, was really not a pleasant one. The first week was great, and we both really enjoyed being there. We saw some of the kids we went to school with, and it again seemed like perhaps I could somehow be one of the "normal" kids.

The next week, however, reality came crashing down on me. Many times in our talks, I have discussed how easy it is for an unthinking adult to harm a child with harsh words. The second week we attended church, a man came up to me to let me know it was not appropriate for me to come to church in blue jeans. Of course, what he didn't know was that I had nothing else to wear and those were the best jeans I had. He also didn't seem to care that it crushed both my sister and me and embarrassed us in front of our peers as well as adults, specifically the one who had invited us. It took many years and much prodding of my Christian friends before I could ever overcome that eventful day. My thought as a child was, if this is what Christians are like, I am not sure I want to be one.

Isn't it disheartening that similar scenarios happen today in our churches, schools and in social settings where children and even sometimes adults are treated like they are somehow inferior to those around them? Years later Lee learned from this experience when he became an active member of the Christian community, but after hearing this story I wonder how many have been turned away from church doors by such individuals as the one who chastised Lee for his outward appearance.

Days on the Farm

It would be too simplistic to conclude that the experience at church that day instigated Lee to withdraw into himself, but it surely was just another brick in the wall Lee had built around himself to keep the outside world away. This world was one where he was safe, secure and could glean joy from his stark surroundings. Listening to Lee relate these stories just made me more and more grateful that I had taken him on as a "project." It also began to paint the picture of a survivor who was going to do whatever he had to do to make it in the world he was given.

At one point in our conversations, Lee told me he was able to be totally alone in crowds. I couldn't, at that point, understand what he was saying, but I am now convinced this coping mechanism began when the family still lived on the Slaughter farm very early in Lee's life. Lee was isolated by his demographics, but he was also able to mentally isolate himself from his surroundings. He told me several stories of how he lived and coped, but the following is again a clue to his inmost feelings and the process by which he learned to survive:

When we lived on the Slaughter place I had many pets — lots of cats, and one special dog. His name was Corky. Corky was a beautiful Cocker Spaniel, and I have to say, at that time in my life he was my only real friend. I have had many pets since that time, but none that I ever connected with like this special dog. It probably had more to do with what I was living through than the dog, but he became a huge comfort to me.

The dog seemed to be able to read my mind and was never away from my side each time I left the house. I had an old BB gun that someone had thrown away which only shot on a random basis. I would walk outside the door with my gun, and Corky would begin to bark and head for the gate that led to the woods in the back of the property.

We would go back there and stay for what seemed like hours, and I would daydream of what my life was going to be when I got older and about having the same things other kids did. My dreams at that point were pretty small and simplistic. If I could just grow up, have a nice family and nice home, I would have made it! I would be able to escape into this dream world of the Beaver Cleaver type family and would only be brought reluctantly back to reality when my mother or my sister would call me back to the house.

The woods at Slaughter's farm where Lee escaped with his dog.

This ability to withdraw into a fantasy world Lee developed at this early age was evidently valuable to him through his formative years in being able to mentally remove himself from his surroundings and place himself in a world known only to him. This skill also allowed Lee to appear to be in total control of a situation, while underneath the surface he was hurting, unsure and alone—alone even in a crowd. The problem with being able to be alone even in a crowd is that one spends much of his or her life in emotional isolation.

10

Not Just Outsiders Tear Down

I NEED TO BE SURE it is understood that it was not just outsiders like the man at church who seemed to be tearing this young Lee down. He related another situation while still in the country where his brother's school club was sponsoring an activity. Lee would be pitted against another boy about his same age in a boxing match. He somehow drew the name of his closest neighbor on a farm down the road. He knew the boy and had convinced himself, with the help of his father and brother, that the contest would be easy. The problem was that the neighbor evidently had not read Lee's press clippings and soundly defeated him.

That would have been bad enough for this fragile child, but his father clearly let him know how disappointed he was in his performance and how he had shamed everyone by not defeating the boy from down the road. After all, the neighbor was heavy and slow and should have been an easy mark. Not only was Lee humiliated by the defeat, but he was also humiliated by the response from his father. Rather than consoling his son and helping him learn from defeat, he taught his son that not winning was unacceptable.

Again listening to Lee showed me the errors many make not only as fathers, but as educators and coaches. I was just at my grandson's baseball game the other day and watched a father/coach scream at eight- and nine-year-old boys like they were supposed to be professionals. I wanted to talk to him and try to let him know what he was doing to those kids, but that was not possible. What was refreshing, however, was watching my son be encouraging towards those same kids. Maybe the time he spent watching and learning from Lee's life has had a positive effect on him. Not only has Lee helped himself, but others as well.

Another Move

As I write this part of Lee's story I find myself in very stark surroundings on a small college campus in Illinois. My wife and I are attending a Fellowship of Christian Athletes leadership camp and have been housed in a student apartment. It has a very small kitchen, two very small bedrooms and to say it has seen hard wear from the students is a gross understatement. I have been struck by the similarities of the way Lee described his new duplex.

For whatever reason, the family had to move from the Slaughter farm. The worn down, unpainted, cold house had become Lee's home, and he told me how devastated he was when he found out they had to move. As was always the case, however, Lee had to find a way to cope, so he rationalized how great it was going to be to move to town. Forget the fact he was moving to the only multifamily dwelling in the town and the fact he was moving in beside an old, old woman who did not like children in the least; he would be in town where he could make new friends.

Once the move took place, however, Lee soon realized he could not continue to rationalize his surroundings. He was now living in the very worst place in town, and everyone knew it. Lee spent a great deal of time describing the new place and how the family had to live:

To understand how awful this move was, I really need to tell you about the house we left. The Slaughter house was in the country and had a big yard, a barn, an old garage and a chicken house. It had little paint but seemed very roomy inside. There was a kitchen, large living room downstairs and two bedrooms. It also had an upstairs where there were three rooms: a bedroom just as you came up the stairway, a small bedroom on the right and then a storage room we called the East Room. This room doubled as a place to play imaginary games when it was too cold or rainy to go outside. I could go outside and run, scream, climb the peach tree and be totally at peace and totally alone.

Of course, the furniture was sparse with no carpet on the floors, but it seemed we had plenty of room. For me it had seemed we had lived there forever, and it was my home. I had my special places where I could go to escape, like the woods and the secret places in the hayloft of the barn where no one could find me.

It was really tough to find anything positive or happy about the move to town. The half of the double we moved into was designed in a straight line. A very small living room was in the front of the house, then one bedroom all three children had to somehow share, another small bedroom where my mom and dad slept and then a very small kitchen. It had no yard to speak of and set just to the side of a large vacant lot that separated us from the local gas station. There were only a couple of trees at the back of the house, but no place for a kid to play and most assuredly no place to escape reality.

During this time I tried to get away as much as possible, and sometimes I could talk my way into spending some time with my best friend Paul. He lived in a nice home in the country, and his mom and dad were very nice to me. Looking back, it is evident that Arlene, Paul's mom, knew my circumstances because she would always encourage me to stay an extra day. I never ever, however, had Paul come to my house.

It is hard to have any positive memories of this time period. I have heard people say that they were poor, but didn't realize it because everyone else was living just like them. That is not the case here. We were poor, and it was evident we were poorer than anyone else. It also seemed that this move caused it to be easier for my dad to get alcohol, and it was at this time I began to see it more and more affect our lives.

Evidence of Change

FROM AN EDUCATOR'S POINT OF VIEW, this move was a much more important event than Lee or any in his family may have been able to comprehend. When talking with Lee and reviewing the notes taken over several years, it was evident it was the beginning of a really tough period for the family—even tougher than the years before.

The most compelling evidence to this fact was twofold. On one hand, Lee and his sister both began to gain significant amounts of weight. At the same time Lee's father seemed to sink deeper and deeper into the influence of alcohol.

Again it seems paradoxical to say the family was more and more desperate while the children got heavier and heavier, but one has to look past the outward appearance and see what kinds of food were being consumed to see the unhealthy lifestyle these two children were living, a lifestyle that is still having a negative effect on both.

It is evident why two of three children began to "fill out," so to speak. Not only were Lee and his sister left alone for extended periods of time, but also the kinds of food they were consuming would quickly add the pounds. A diet heavy on starches was available and taken advantage of throughout the day. Lee recounted that raw potatoes with much salt was a staple when it came to snacks. The potatoes were cheap and easy to get, so many were consumed. Likewise, it was easy to get stale bread. Lee and his sister consumed huge amounts of bread on a daily basis. Even though it is hard for those who have never lived through something like this to understand, Lee reported that he and his sister would consume at least an entire loaf of bread each morning. They, of course, had no toaster, but they would put the bread into an oven, toast it on one side, turn it over and toast it on the other. He said they would then take it out, load it with butter and jelly and sit in front of one of their new best friends, the TV, and cheerfully consume it all. It is evident to see why the weight began to accumulate on both the younger children.

The older brother was not in that same mode. Because he was older, he was able to get away from the confines of the duplex and work on his own. When asked, Lee could not remember his older brother being around much during those times. He was old enough to drive and work on farms, so Lee reasons he probably slept at the duplex, but that was about all.

12

The Downward Spiral

IT WAS ALSO DURING THIS TIME IN LEE'S LIFE that he began to really realize the depths of his father's problem with alcohol and the direct effects of it. Before, Lee knew his dad drank but really did not link the drinking to the issues the family faced on a daily basis. Lee knew his family didn't have much but had not reasoned that if his father hadn't been drinking, they could have perhaps had more than they did.

Lee was at approximately the third grade level, and just as educators realize, students usually figure out about this time where they really stand as far as their intelligence level and status in comparison to others. Lee figured out that one of the main differences between him and his peers was that their fathers weren't spending abnormal amounts of time in the local tavern. Events at this time of Lee's life had a devastating effect on his relationship with his father. His father probably didn't realize it or mean to do it, but actions he took adversely affected his impressionable son. Lee recalls this era:

My sister and I spent a lot of time by ourselves really from just before we left the Slaughter farm. She mothered me and took care of me and made sure I was fed. There was a problem in that we did not have healthy diets and we both began to gain weight. We had nothing to do, no place to go, no friends to play with, no place to play, nothing to play with, so we were basically stuck in the cramped, drab, small duplex watching TV and eating ourselves into problems. Food became our comfort and escape from our everyday life.

While Mom and Dad both had to work to make ends meet, we were the ones who chose to consume the amounts of food we did. The reality of the fact is, however, the food filled a void we both had in our lives.

At about this time a dreaded weekend routine began to happen, and it happened so often, it had an everlasting effect on me, one that I am still trying to get over. On Saturday mornings my dad would tell my mom he and I were going somewhere. (I was never privy to those conversations.) Where we would end up was, I am sure, not where he told Mom we were going. There was no tavern in our town, so he would load his young son into the family car and head to the tavern in the nearby town. He would park the car on the side of the street and assure me he would be "right back."

I would sit for hours in the car by myself. If someone would have seen and realized what was happening, my father could surely have been in trouble, but I was resourceful and embarrassed. I can remember lying down in the floor of the car so no one could see me. I felt as if everyone knew where my dad was, and I was devastated by having to be there.

I can remember sitting for a long time and becoming so fearful and frustrated that I would go to the front of the tavern and try to look inside the heavily tinted windows to see if I could get my dad's attention to try and convince him to leave. After failing to do so, I would run back to the car and jump in to hide again, fearing that one of my friends from school might see me.

Every so often Dad would come walking down the alley with steadily increasing difficulty and hand me a Coke. That was supposed to make it all better and he would again tell me he would be right back and he would head back to his haven of safety, his buddies at the bar. I have never been able to rationalize this behavior on my dad's part. As a kid his actions were telling me that the alcohol and his friends in the tavern were more important than his son in the car. I must forgive, but have trouble forgetting.

The lonely place where Lee's father parked the car and left young Lee during tavern visits.

Lee's father would momentarily break the long hours of isolation when he would stagger down this alley to bring Lee a Coke.

Seeing the tavern where his father drank brings back feelings of pain and loneliness for Lee.

It's hard to swallow that a father would do something like this to his son, just as it is disturbing that many adults—educators, clergy, and parents—still put children in similar situations and don't realize the effects it can have. No, perhaps they don't leave children in cars by themselves, but adults may leave them isolated in a classroom, in the lunchroom, at home or at church, put aside emotionally if not physically, and never realize or care that they are doing damage from which children may never fully recover.

My mind went back to experiences with my own children. Had there been times when I unknowingly isolated them and made them feel abandoned or afraid? From their innocent perspective, were they ever made to feel shut out from the safety of my love and protection? I thought of times when perhaps I brushed them off because I was too busy with my own concerns to acknowledge their need for interaction. Was that not isolating and hurtful as well?

Just as Lee's dad may have changed his behavior if he had realized what it was doing to his son, so too I prayed that myself and those reading Lee's story would think and be aware before they ignore or neglect children in even a subtle way that can adversely affect them.

13

The Thin Thread of Family

READING AND LEARNING ABOUT LEE to this point would make one believe there was nothing or no one positive in his life. That is thankfully not the case.

Two people Lee talked about with great admiration and fond memories were his grandparents on his mother's side. He called them Mom and Papaw. Their real names were Cecil and Betty. I know that because I did know them before their passing. They lived just down the street from the duplex. Cecil was a hard working farm hand, and during this time of Lee's life Cecil worked for a rich gentleman farmer named Otis. Otis owned many farms and much land and was one of those people Lee looked up to as being successful. He drove big cars, lived in a big home and showed his wealth by the way he lived his life.

Otis had money, but he didn't share much with Cecil. Cecil and Betty's home was not fancy by any stretch of imagination, but it was theirs. It sat as the first dwelling past the hardware store and just across from another gas station. The setting was much like the setting of the duplex, just on the opposite side of town: the duplex on the north, their house on the south. The house had some yard and was well kept even though structurally it was not very sound.

Cecil and Betty had a real positive effect on Lee. His memories of them and their home were very pleasant. Cecil was hard working, caring and sometimes ornery. He had a great sense of humor and was known in town as a tough as nails man with a heart of gold. He cared about Lee and showed it in very real ways. Betty did, too, and Lee cherished the time he had with his grandparents:

At probably some of the toughest times in my life, I can remember the great times I had when I went to my grandparents' home. They lived just on the other side of town, and that meant walking like a city block to get to their house.

Mom and Papaw always had time for me and a place at their table. The smell of fresh coffee and biscuits and gravy seemed to welcome me each time I walked into their home. As soon as I would walk through the door, Mom would begin to set me a plate and pour me a cup of coffee. Yes, even at this young age, coffee. Of course it would be three parts milk and sugar and one part coffee, but I was just as much a part of that meal as all the others.

There was just a feeling of being welcome in their home and a caring from them that gave me a sense of belonging. When I walked in the house Mom would immediately begin to see to it that my needs were met. Those were great times, and I knew I was loved.

It was not long before this close relationship and proximity changed. For some reason Otis decided that he no longer needed the services of Cecil, or Cecil decided to move on to bigger and better things. Either way, Cecil and Betty moved to a country farm and Cecil became a tenant farmer. They did not own the land or the home, but did all the farming as if it were theirs. I am not really sure of the acreage he tended, but they seemed happy and probably for the first time in their lives were in control of their own destiny.

A Move to the South Side

Of course, the move of his grandparents was tough on Lee, but there was an up side. The house on the south side that had such great memories for him was now going to be vacant, and his grandparents needed someone to move in and take care of their beloved home. Lee's family was once again moving, but this time it was definitely a move up. They were going to be back in a single-family home—one that had great potential for Lee and his family. After all, it had such great memories and smells attached to it, Lee couldn't see how anything could be negative about the move, especially because they would be escaping from the duplex.

Once again the move created real hope for a better life for all concerned. Once again, however, the hope and better life did not come to reality. It was a different setting, but the problems of the family followed them down the street to the new home. Without his grandparents there, the once safe, warm and aromatic home became much the same as the duplex without the old lady living next door—just a cold, empty house.

Once the family actually moved in, the house took on real characteristics rather than the sentimental memories of a small boy who visited on occasion. Lee saw the house differently once he was there all the time. It is much like in life when we see appealing things from afar; once we get closer to the object of desire, it may not be quite as attractive as it initially appeared.

The house on South Main

The home was small, the floors uneven and the house was cold. There was no insulation, and in the winter, the wind could be seen moving the curtains around the windows. The upstairs was small and cramped, and getting upstairs seemed like a risky venture. Lee remembered the stairs being much steeper than typical staircases and actually scary to try to climb to get to the drab, musty, dirty rooms. The bedroom where Lee was housed with his brother actually had a cracked window that was never repaired the entire time the family lived there.

The house needed to be painted and repaired, but his grandparents simply did not have the money or the inclination to do so. The wooden siding was supposed to be white but had grayed and faded. The boards took on an erratic appearance where some looked to have paint and others looked as though they were still waiting on the first long awaited color to be applied. It also was a sure bet that Lee's parents would not have the money nor would they spend it to fix a house that was not theirs.

Of course, there were good times, and positive things happened, but again it seemed the grossly negative outweighed the positive. Lee did begin to have people in his life who showed an interest in him and what he did. His sister was always there, but after this move he also began to play organized sports for the first time, and the men who coached him must have seen something in him because they seemed to take special care in the way he was treated. His first sport was Little League baseball, and he instantly found some success. Since Lee was so heavy, however, his position quickly became catcher where his lack of foot speed would not hinder him as much.

The negatives of poverty and alcohol abuse continued to escalate along with his weight and the emotional baggage he seemed to be accumulating. A heavy withdrawal from his emotional bank account happened one hot Saturday afternoon after Lee's mother had gone to pick up her cancelled checks from the local bank. As Lee was relating this incident it was evident what a profound effect it had on him and probably his sister as well:

Not long after we had moved into our grandparents' home in the south end of town, the only time that I can remember my father being abusive to my mom occurred. It was on a summer Saturday, and Mom had been to the bank to pick up her cancelled checks to balance the checkbook. As was the norm for this time in our lives and for years afterward, Dad had written checks for alcohol and had not bothered to let Mom know. She confronted him at a bad time, Saturday, when he still had plenty of alcohol to consume as well as having already consumed plenty before the confrontation.

Mom was very astute and did not want my sister and me to be subjected to this particular battle, so she sent us outside to await the outcome. We really never thought too much about it because it happened many times before. Mom would confront, Dad would apologize, and then all would be right with the world until the next month.

This time, though, there was something different. My sister and I were not part of the conversation, but from where we were standing, we could see into the kitchen window where the battle was about to commence. Again it was not all that frightening ... that is, until we saw my dad place his hands around my mother's neck. At that point rather than being frightened or just condoning this act, I ran into the house and shouted, and Dad backed away. He never before had been mean when intoxicated, and I don't ever remember him doing anything like that again, but on that day I realized how blessed we were that he wasn't typically physically abusive when he drank.

This event affected me so much that I can still remember it like it was yesterday. I still think about it often after all these years, and looking back now how thankful I am my dad was the way he was even in the bad times. It could have been so much worse. He could have been mean and violent to us like so many others with the same type of alcohol problem, but he wasn't. Overall, Pop was a good man...a good man who had serious problems.

I could not believe the level of insight and maturity Lee displayed. Although he was obviously deeply hurt by his father's actions, he was still able to take a step back and attempt to understand his father and to see him for what he really was... a man with problems. So many in life are not so sympathetic or forgiving as Lee. As I listened to Lee I began to consider the people in my life who dealt with such problems as alcoholism and other addictions. I felt a wellspring of compassion rising up in me for those whose lives had fallen prey to so many of the world's traps. Would I be as compassionate as Lee were I in his shoes?

Lee related another story that reinforced the serious nature of his family's financial problems. He remembered his family sitting in the kitchen at his grandparents' home when someone knocked on the door. When his dad opened the door, the man standing there in a suit was not there for the good of the family—that was evident. He was visible to young Lee as well as being within earshot, so the entire family could overhear the short conversation between the well-dressed man and the father. The man was there to repossess something that had been purchased on credit and subsequently not been paid for.

Lee's dad was no small person and quickly sent the man on his way. His dad came back to the table visibly upset but tried to comfort his wife and the rest of the family. Lee remembered vividly that he soon heard a noise over his shoulder and turned to see the man now standing in the back door into the kitchen. His dad leapt to his feet, and the man was escorted roughly out the way he came in. Lee never knew what the man was after, but could not remember anything missing from the home in the subsequent days. It was events like this that made Lee understand what the drinking was doing to the family financially and why his mother acted the way she did when it came to the family finances.

Some Insights

FOOD, FAITH, EDUCATORS, LEADERS, friends, family, and those negative events of life all show up in Lee's early life and those same threads continue to form the fabric of the rest of his life as well. You are getting a clearer and clearer picture of who this young man was and how he got to where he was the day he walked into my class at approximately 12 years of age.

It should be noted that there really are two kinds of poverty Lee suffered through his life: financial and emotional. We should always realize neither of these is acceptable, but we must also realize that just because a person is poor, it doesn't mean that they cannot have a joyful and happy life. That is just not true! I recently read a book by a former NFL player, Don McNeal, who lived in severe economic poverty through most of his life and was happy and fulfilled all through his childhood. This is an example of emotional wealth in the midst of financial poverty.

Likewise, I have a friend who has more wealth than most can ever imagine, but his children are emotionally poverty stricken because he has spent his whole adult life chasing the dollar rather than building emotional wellness in his family. The bottom line is that money or the lack of money is not the cause of emotional wealth or poverty. It is much more than that; it is what people and experience deposit into a person's life.

Family Members

As Lee and I were talking, I asked him if he would spend some time going back in his memory to give me as specifically as he could a profile of his nuclear family members. The reason I wanted him to do this was to see how, if any, his descriptions would change from those I had remembered from our conversations early in his life. I encouraged him to give as much detail as he could remember. The descriptions you will read here will be in Lee's own words. I asked if he would go in reverse order of age and discuss each person: his older sister, his older brother, his mother and his father. I asked him to try to recall what his family was like around the time we first met.

Sister

My sister Sue is four years older than me. So at the time you asked me to describe, she would have been 12 or 13. At this time she and I had both begun to put on weight, but what I remember most about her was how much she mothered me. To put a girl of her age in the position of having to totally take care of her little brother was not fair at all. She had no time to be a little girl and was forced to grow up way too soon.

Sue was and is a beautiful person. She has a lovely face and smile and loving, caring eyes. As she matured she had very attractive dark hair and a dark complexion.

She seemed not to have many close friends outside of the family. At one point she shared with me that she enjoyed getting "away" and going to spend time with our aunt and uncle in a nearby town. I really don't have the desire to tell you how strange that would seem to many. That house that she liked to go to was one of the dirtiest and filled with odor. It was one of the worst places I have ever been in. I personally couldn't stand to go there for any reason. That does show how really unhappy and unappreciated my wonderful sister felt.

You would have to ask her, but I recall that she did much of the cooking for the family. Especially in the summer months when we would be home all day by ourselves, she was expected to have the dinner ready for the rest of the family when they got home from work.

It saddens me that as adults my sister and I hardly ever talk. I have never taken the time to thank her for all she did for me, and frankly I hadn't really thought that much about it until you asked me to do this. I believe she is very bitter about our life and the way she was treated, and as I have gone through the thought process for this activity, I think I can understand some of her bitterness.

I'll share one specific example of how she took care of me, or at least did her best to do so. I was playing baseball in a vacant lot between the hardware and the TV repair shop. In the summer months we were allowed to go without shoes, and I was actually playing baseball barefoot. Of course this was extremely stupid and dangerous, and while crossing the plate after a long home run off the wall of the TV shop, I stepped on a piece of broken glass and nearly severed my big toe on my right foot.

I limped home, bleeding all the way, and ran to my sister for help. She calmly sat me down in a chair in the kitchen and began her Florence Nightingale impersonation to nurse me back to health. Being 12, she administered first aid to the best of her knowledge and ability and with the supplies she had at hand. She carefully placed a basin under my foot and poured rubbing alcohol on the open gash. The pain was unbelievable! But she probably saved me more pain of infection by her actions. She then dressed the wound, put me on the couch and elevated my foot to keep it from bleeding more until my parents got home.

My sister was great to me, and I just wish we could be as close now as we were during our childhood.

Brother

My brother Bus is eight years older than me, and when we were growing up, I always looked up to him. He was strong and well built, and his good looks made it easy for him to be with the best looking girls in school. He was always clean-cut and well dressed, and he seemed to have it all together. He was a great athlete for his school and was in basketball, baseball and track ... He actually set the school record for the 100 dash his senior year, a record that stood for eight years before it was broken. Like my sister, he seemed to have the dark complexion of my father, and my brother didn't have any of the weight problems my sister and I had. He spent many hours working for the local farmers. At one time he even worked on a milk route where he picked up milk from dairy farmers in the area. The fact he worked much of his time helped, I am sure, keep himself in shape and also kept him isolated from all the bad stuff that was happening with me and my sister

For all outward appearances, he was the "golden boy." I think this adversely affected my sister more than me, but many times I remember it seeming as though he got much more than either of us. I think the whole family looked up to him, and I believe Dad lived vicariously through my brother's accomplishments for most of his high school years.

I could just never imagine my brother ever doing anything wrong, and I think that's the same way my mom and dad felt. My brother and I had to sleep in the same room ... I can remember him coming home late and I could smell cigarette smoke on him. I would convince myself that it had to be the people he was with because he would never smoke.

Since my brother was older, he wasn't around much. He worked, dated, played sports so he was rarely home. He mainly used the house as a place to sleep, not live. I don't believe my brother would remember our life being that bad, and I think that makes sense since he wasn't there to see and experience what my sister and I saw and lived through.

He was four years older than my sister, so he was 17 or so when we lived at the house on South Main. We lived there when another life changing event took place. It was right after he had graduated from high school and had gone to work in the same factory where my dad worked. I could tell there was tension in the house ... even more than usual. I came in one day after they got home from work to see my brother sitting at the kitchen table smoking a cigarette. This was devastating to me to see my hero puffing away on a Camel cigarette. I assumed this was why every-one had been acting so strange, but pretty soon I found out that wasn't the reason.

My family had been trying to protect me from the truth, but I soon realized a new member was coming into the family. My brother was going to be married and would soon be living in a small trailer behind the house on South Main. No one expected this, and he and his fiancée were just 18, but it was to happen nonetheless. I could easily sense the families were not happy about the situation, and the golden boy seemed to be a bit tarnished.

My brother and I still talk with each other at times and see each other. I can't say we're close, but there's a connection between us because after his first marriage ended tragically after 38 years, he ended up marrying my sister-in-law. It is a bit odd, but this at least keeps us in touch with each other.

Mother

My mother was then and still is one of the strongest women I've ever known. She stands only around five feet tall, but her character and personality make her seem much taller. At this time in my life, it was my mom who held our frag-ile family together. She worked hard every day of her life, and I am sure during this period the money she brought home was all that kept us from the creditors and from going hungry.

Mom was a very attractive and small lady who seemed a lot larger than her small frame showed. She had dish-water blonde hair and a laugh that could fill a room with joy. Those moments were not as often as they should have been or she deserved, but she had a wonderful smile—a smile I believe my sister inherited from her.

Even though my dad was large and intimidating, I was much more frightened of my mother. She could dress you down like no other human being I have ever been around. She had a way with words and facial expressions that made even the strongest of men and women who tried to cross her cringe and withdraw.

At times this fireball of a lady could burn someone even though they may not have deserved it. I can remember times when she would be worried over our financial situation (which was most of the time), and the paper boy would come to the door to collect for his deliveries of the week before. My mom would carefully check, and if she could find no evidence to her liking, she would launch into the poor unsuspecting youth and give him a lesson in proper record keeping that I am sure he wouldn't soon forget.

Mom did not go to church, and I'm not sure at this time if she was a Christian, but she did display many Christian principles in her everyday life. She honored her marriage vows, and during times when she could have thrown my father out and no one would have blamed her, she stuck to her promise and loved him through the bad times. She later in life loved him through sickness just as she had promised on her wedding day.

Looking back now, I believe Mom was an enabler because she always protected my dad and made excuses for his behavior. She would never ever think of smoking or drinking herself, but she allowed and excused the abuse of both by Dad. She also allowed my father's emotional abuse to all of us kids, especially my sister.

Father

It should be no surprise that I don't have many good memories of my father from this time you are asking me to remember. Dad was a big man, much bigger in my mind than he actually was. He was actually about six foot one or two. He was overweight at this time and continued the rest of his life to get larger. One of the reasons was that he'd get up during the night and literally eat anything that was in the refrigerator. This usually happened when he wasn't thinking since he was under the influence of alcohol.

As I look back at pictures of Dad and view them objectively—not through the lens of a hurt kid—Dad was a handsome man. He had dark eyes, a dark complexion and hair black as coal until later in life. He often sported a thin mustache that many said made him look even more distinguished. Seeing pictures of him during his time in the Navy, he was well built and strong, much like my older brother. Because Dad and my brother looked so much alike in their youth, it probably makes sense that Dad could relate to him better than my sister and me.

During this time his drinking kept getting worse and worse, and he never seemed to have much drive to succeed or make his life any better. He seemed content to scrape out a meager living and live in other people's houses and drive old cars. He did not maintain good personal hygiene. Maybe it was because of our living conditions, but I don't remember anyone else in the family having odor, but I do remember that with him.

One positive thing about him though was he never

missed work. Every day he would get up and go to his job at the factory, and his drinking did not cause him to miss. After studying the effects of alcohol and the disease itself, I would say he was a classic weekend alcoholic. I don't mean that he only drank on the weekends, but he at least did not allow the drinking to cause him to lose his job, and he hid his addiction from many he dealt with on a daily basis.

Dad also had skills that others recognized and utilized. He was a welder, and many called on him to weld and repair when others couldn't get the job done. It is sad that he was talented in so many ways, but never ever used his talents to improve life for us.

A Bit of Analysis

WHILE LISTENING TO LEE discuss his family and recalling my notes from his reflections as a 12 year old, I was struck with the strength of the women in his life. He remembered his sister and his mother both being strong, basically the cement that held the family together. While both his male role models seemed to disappoint and let him down, his female role models were steadfast, had servant's hearts and were resilient in times of adversity.

It is also noteworthy to point out that Lee's father had skills which he could possibly have used to bring his family out of the financial poverty. However, perhaps because of his own emotional poverty, Lee's dad perpetuated both types of poverty in his own family.

Another House, Another Chance
It was hard to believe, but Lee moved to the sixth house he remembered living in and he was still not yet 12 years old. This was another rental property in the same small town and was

farther south. It was, as a matter of fact, directly across the street from the church where Lee and his sister had the unpleasant experience he spoke of earlier.

The house was a bit better than those he had lived in before, and he really didn't have any explanation as to how the step up happened. It was still one of the less desirable homes, but a far cry from the duplex where they lived when they first came to town.

As Lee opened up about this house, I found out things he had never shared with me before. Although it was hard for him to bring back the memories, it was another glimpse inside this very complicated man whom I thought I knew better than anyone else.

The house was one story with a bedroom in the front where Lee slept, a living room, a bedroom where his mother and father slept, and a bedroom for his sister. His brother had gone to live in the country with his new wife and now new child, so Lee's nuclear family was now four. The kitchen was small as were all the rooms, but the outside of the house had paint and looked fairly normal. The inside of the house was not much different than others as it had only cheap linoleum on the floors and the walls had long needed paint.

There was an old barn on the back of the property that bordered some open fields, and Lee said he had pleasant memories of playing basketball by himself using the goal on the side of the barn. It was like watching a scene from the movie *Hoosiers* as I listened to him tell of scraping snow off the ground so he could shoot hoops in the middle of winter. You could almost see him reliving this moment as he explained he always wore gloves, if he could find any, because someone had told him that would make him a better player if he could learn to handle the basketball while wearing gloves.

Lee's mood quickly changed, however, as did his countenance when I asked him how the family was doing during this quick stay at house number six. He began to have a very different look in his eyes when he began to recall memories that were evidently very painful. It seems that his father's drinking had worsened even more, and his memories of this particular house and the events that took place while they lived there were some of the worst. This was probably the reason he had not shared them with me when he was younger. During the early years of our relationship, he had learned how to mask the pain and hurt through laughter and achievement. Now, when he was older it was easier to let down his guard and speak from his heart.

Lee shared a particular hurtful event that occurred the first Christmas the family experienced at the house on South Main. He had spotted a football uniform, complete with pants, shirt, helmet and kicking tee in the window at the hardware store. He had gone by several times just to look at it and dream that someday he could have one just like it. With Christmas coming up he thought he might have a chance, so he pleaded and begged to his mother and father that it would be the best Christmas ever if he could just have that uniform.

One could only imagine the hope and yearning in a young boy's mind and heart that maybe, just this once, for the first time in his life, he would get what he had asked for—and the threatening possibility that he likely tried to suppress of the crushing disappointment he would face if that wonderful football uniform was not under the tree that morning. Lee shares that memory with you:

I had really convinced myself that when I got up on Christmas morning that the football uniform would be under the tree for all to see and for me to enjoy. I really had no reason to believe it would be there based on past Christmas disappointments, but all children have that hope that we as adults seem to lose.

As I carefully opened the door from my bedroom to gaze longingly at the Christmas tree ... there it was!! The only gift that could possibly have made my Christmas the most special ever was waiting for me to enjoy. I literally began to cry and could not contain my excitement. I rushed to the tree, tore open the box and began to touch and experience the best gift I had ever received! I tore off my pajamas and began to finalize this most special occasion by putting on my gift, when the joy quickly turned to devastation.

I really don't know what happened, and no one ever took the time to explain to me, but it was evident no one had thought of looking at the size of the gift and the comparable size of the boy. As I had told you before, I had gained a lot of weight, and when I tried to put the football pants on, I could barely get them past my knees. Instead of consoling or helping, there was laughter. I can remember the laughter that here this fat little boy couldn't get his football pants on. With that hurt ingrained in my head and now the tears flowing because of embarrassment rather than joy, the jersey and pads were to go on. The shoulder pads were held together with a shoestring, so I was able to pull them out far enough they could go over my shoulders (barely), and then it was time for the black Chicago Bears jersey to go over the pads. Of course if the pants were too small, I don't know why I or anyone else thought the jersey would fit, and it didn't.

In my memory no one ever tried to explain or apologize for the gift and the subsequent pain I felt. I do know that the uniform was never exchanged, and the only thing I was able to play with from it was the kicking tee and the helmet. It was just another of those events that at that time of my life made me believe that I was not worth much, not even the time to care.

The Depth of Despair

It is intriguing to me how God works and puts experiences and timing into our lives to make things crystal clear. Just the other night as I was sitting in a hotel in Florida waiting to work a show for one of our companies, I was watching a documentary television show about drinking and especially about the different types of vodka. Having never been a drinker myself, it really brought clarity to my thought process about what Lee had told me of his father's drinking while they lived on South Main.

In the show they defined vodka as a colorless, odorless and tasteless drink. They went into its history a bit, and the James Bond movies were the ones that made drinking vodka the "in thing" to do. In the documentary, they conducted a taste test, and none of the participants could pick out the vodka of their choice even though they thought before they started they would easily be able to do so. It was also stated by all the experts that virtually no one drank vodka straight; it was almost always used in a mixed drink, which caused it to be even harder to distinguish between the different brands.

The reason I share this bit of information is to underscore the depths to which Lee's father had gone during this time. Lee knew his dad drank too much, but not knowing the facts on vodka, Lee only had his view of his father, not that of any experts.

Lee shared with me that his father would come home every single night with a half-pint of vodka and six cans of beer. Knowing now that hardly anyone drinks vodka straight, Lee's memory of his father is even more telling. Lee shared that his dad would get a large glass, pour the vodka into the glass, and then proceed to drink the entire glass at one time. He would do that with consecutive glasses until he had "chugged" the entire bottle. He would then proceed to drink all six cans of beer in quick succession. Of course, by the time he ate his dinner, he would pass out on the couch and be there until he woke up to stagger to bed. Lee remembers this to be a nightly ritual. His father would be intoxicated all through the weekend until he ran out of his "stash" he had purchased on Friday and Saturday.

Lee already revealed that his mother and father would have their worst fights when the bank statement came and his father would have the family in dire straights because he had written checks and not informed his wife. After another fight, Lee experienced something no child at that age should have had to experience, but it was but another time when it was evident God was looking over him and his family even though none were walking in the Christian faith:

My dad was drinking more and more. He also tended to gamble way too much, especially since we hardly had enough money to eat, let alone gamble any away. Maybe he thought he could hit it big and get us out of the situation we were in, but it never happened, and we sank deeper and deeper as he sank deeper and deeper into escape through alcohol. Of course, to gamble and drink he was taking money from our checking account and not even letting Mom know, and each time the bank statements came there would be another battle.

Dad tried to rationalize both habits, and on occasion he would win something or some money. On one such occasion he came home proudly with a Remington Nylon 66 automatic rifle. It was an impressive gun and the only one we ever had in the house that I can remember. I don't know why, but he always kept the gun under the bed in my bedroom in the front of the house.

After one particularly volatile fight over the lack of funds in the checkbook, dad had his usual nightly drink. Before he passed out, I was standing in the living room and realized the door to my bedroom was shut and Dad was nowhere to be seen. I've never had the blessing of having God speak to me audibly, but something told me to open the door to my bedroom. It was not like a feeling; it was more like a demand. As I threw open the door, my dad was sitting on the side of my bed with the Remington Nylon 66 between his legs, the barrel to the middle of his forehead, and his thumb on the trigger. As I tell you this now, I can see it vividly as if I were there again. I lunged toward him and knocked the gun away and yelled at him. It must have startled him enough that he realized what he was doing, and he calmly got up, went to the couch and passed out. As was the norm in our family, nothing was discussed about the incident, and it was as if it never happened the next morning.

It is telling and sad that this boy had to go through what he did without much help from anyone. The fact is that many today are living through the same if not worse situations, and many of us just choose to live our lives in our own comfortable worlds and put those like Lee out of our minds.

I began to think back on all the children I had encountered as an educator. I wondered if I had missed any clues, overlooked any signs of lives lived in volatile circumstances. I felt a heavy sadness for Lee and the children like him who were wounded daily by the very people who should have been loving and protecting them. If not the parents, then who?

I am sure if people would take the time to observe and care for children and adults going through tough times, the pain could be lessened by simply showing compassion. Perhaps by caring and sharing, we could keep so many from failure and some ultimately from the correctional institutions our society seems eager to put them. "Tail them, nail them and jail them" seems to be the mindset in our country rather than "Know them, love them and help them."

16

Another Move ... and Then We Meet

THE STAY AT SOUTH MAIN was not long, but again it was enough time to have several issues that Lee had to live through and learn to cope with. He shared that he was actively playing little league baseball and had done so since he was seven years old. Since Lee lived in a very small town, he found himself playing catcher in every game. (Isn't that where all little fat boys end up?)

Right before the family moved again, Lee was experiencing much pain in his knees, especially his right one. It was much worse after he played a baseball game and, as was the norm in his family, he was told he would be fine and to *"suck it up and act like a man."* Finally, after the last game, Lee's knees were so bad he could not get out of the car when the family came home after yet another game where he was placed as catcher.

After much arguing and discussion, Lee's mother finally won, and Lee was reluctantly taken to the doctor. Upon examination and X-rays, the doctor diagnosed Lee with a condition that caused him to have his right knee put in a cast. Again there was never any apology to the young boy and no discussion, just life as usual the next day.

The move to Wall Street was again a joyful experience. Even though the house was filthy dirty both inside and out from the previous renters, it was a sound house with plenty of room and a huge bathroom—only one for the entire family, but at least one that worked. The house was a two-story, and with the older brother long gone, it was very sufficient for the family of four.

Lee explained how excited the family was once again to be moving and starting over, and how he and his sister went to the house and thoroughly cleaned both the inside and out before the family moved in. The old siding needed painting, but again since the family was only renting, the paint wasn't going to happen, so Lee and his sister spent hours washing the outside of the house with soap and water. Although still dull and grey, at least the house was much more appealing than it was before the labor from the two young kids.

The house on Wall Street

The home was much like the others Lee and his family had lived in, with no carpet, walls that needed painting, and floors that were uneven, but it was still a move up in the minds of the family members. The kitchen was a large room but had no cabinets, and the sink was old and stained. There were two front doors, one leading into the kitchen and one leading into the large living room. There were two back doors, one off the kitchen and one off the dining room that set between the kitchen and living room. The back porch was old, dilapidated and had an old building attached that at some time had been used as a storage area for coal. The yard was in need of being mowed in some places and bare of any grass in many other areas. It seemed obvious to Lee that those who had rented before his family did not care what the house looked like inside and out.

Again in this house there were three bedrooms—two upstairs and one downstairs. Lee and his sister's rooms were upstairs, and his mother and father's bedroom was just off the bathroom. The woodwork was old and in many places the paint was flaking off the walls as well as the woodwork. This sounds like a very sad place to live, but as Lee was explaining the surroundings, it was as if he and his family were moving into a mansion on Wall Street rather than a run-down rental in need of many repairs.

This house was to become special to Lee's family. Not only did they live there all the time I knew his family, but it was the first house Lee's mother and father ever bought. They had lived in the home for a few years, and the landlord gave them the chance to purchase the home on contract. Of course, the family jumped at the opportunity, and once they had ownership, they began systematically to make it their own and spend time and what little money they could spare to fix it up and make it livable. It was at about this same time that I first met Lee.

The Early Meetings

That first meeting I discussed earlier still sticks in my mind like many other significant events in my life—my wedding day, the birth of my children. It was as if it was yesterday, and the impact Lee had on me and continues to have on me has never changed.

I would like to give you, the reader, a small glimpse of what I experienced that first meeting. Words can't do it justice, but I will try and explain why this child was so out of the ordinary.

Lee came into my classroom and sat patiently at his desk. He was wearing jeans that were old even though this was the first day of school and most all other children in his class were in their new stiff jeans and new shirts. Lee's looked like they could have used a good washing, and there was a good bit of him hanging over the side of the jeans that were evidently too small for his rather plump body. His shirt was untucked in an evident attempt to cover the excess skin that was showing, and it gaped at the buttons as they strained to keep the shirt together where his body was pushing hard trying to escape the confines of the well-worn fabric.

He seemed to be clean as far as his body was concerned, but his dishwater blonde hair, which was cut in a way that was evidently supposed to be cropped close to his scalp, had grown past the time for a hair cut and was now beginning to hang over his ears, but only slightly. His shoes were well worn, too, and looked as though they were left over from school years past, whether his brother or some other kind soul had given them to him.

He looked like those children you see on television who live in poverty and seemed destined to remain there. To my surprise, when I had my first meeting with him, he jumped up, walked proudly into the office, sat down and had a look like *Now what do you want me to do?* He had an infectious smile that was such a contrast to what I expected with his exterior being so sad. This seeming contradiction was the first hook he had in me. What could cause this fat, unkempt young boy to seem so happy and well adjusted?

I mentioned earlier some of that first conversation and my realization that I knew of his family. This also was the meeting where he let me know in no uncertain terms that he would not end up like his father. It was at this point that I decided I must find out what made this boy tick. We talked for several minutes, and then I asked him if he would mind coming back and talking to me again later in the week. He said that would be fine, and we made our next meeting time the following Friday. In the meantime, I shared the meeting with my wife and told her of my thought of studying this boy named Lee to see if I could learn from him to be able to help others who would be following him through our school. Whether he succeeded or failed in life, I would learn and hopefully from the knowledge gained from Lee, I could help others in my life-long career in education.

17

Teachers' Impacts

A S YOU CAN PROBABLY IMAGINE, I don't have time in the confines of this book to go over every single meeting we had over the years. Some meetings were very uneventful and would not move Lee's story on for you, the reader, and would be a waste of good trees to put the results on the pages of this book. Others, however, had such an impact on me and taught me so much about Lee specifically and children like him, that Lee and I will go into some detail of what transpired in them. The second meeting we had that week was one such meeting.

Again, Lee sat patiently waiting for me to summon him into the confines of the office I had reserved. He came in with the same shoes and I am sure the same pants he had on earlier in the week. The shirt was a different one but with still the same task of concealing the body of this pudgy little boy. It looked as though he had a bit of trim done on his hair, but it was evident he had not been to the barber shop to have it done. He again flashed his smile and opened our conversation with a cheerful, *"What's up?"*

After laughing together for the first of many times to come, we began our journey together in earnest. Since Lee was just coming out of elementary school, I thought it logical to ask him how he liked school and about the teachers he had in elementary. Wow, the results that came from that simple question gave me the first insight into this young man and why he would probably succeed in keeping his covenant of not being like his father. He just lit up when he started talking about his teachers and how much they had meant to him. He could name every teacher from first grade through sixth that he had just left. As he mentioned each, he was able to tell me why each one was special and what he/she had done for him to make him still love school.

His first grade teacher was a woman named Mrs. Young. Lee didn't know her first name, but he could sure remember what she looked like and how special she was. What struck me about Lee's description of Mrs. Young when he was older, and at this meeting as well, was his total understanding that she cared for him. At a time when this boy most certainly needed someone to care, she did.

Lee went on to go slowly through all his teachers, taking the time to comment on each one. From my notes on this meeting, it was evident all were very different and brought many different strengths to the classroom and all had positively impacted this young boy. I believe Lee's experience in his early school years was as unique as he was. To think that a student would have the good fortune to benefit from every one of his teachers is something we all wish could happen to every child who walks through the doors of our schools. It is not to say that all Lee's experiences were wonderful with these teachers, but overall each brought another building block in assuring the future success or at least the opportunity for success for this student.

Lee mentioned all his teachers but he shared two specific events, one from the fifth grade and one from the sixth, that polarized what good experiences and bad experiences can do to a young, impressionable child.

The first occurred in the fifth grade. Although his classroom teacher, Mrs. Harting, had nothing to do with the situation, she probably could have softened the blow had she been more aware of young Lee's family and the trauma of a seemingly unimportant event in his life that adversely affected him for many years.

It seems in the fall of that year, the physical education teacher had decided to put together a track and field team that would compete against other elementary schools in the immediate area. Of course, Lee, coming from the background he did and observing the accolades his athletic older brother received from his father and members of the community, he wanted to be on the team in the worst way. To make it even more important to him, his brother held the high school record in the 100-yard dash, the most glamorous of the track events.

We must remember that Lee was overweight, small and weak at this stage of his life. Also, this school Lee attended fed into the high school where his brother had left his mark as a track star. Equally important is the fact that this track team was designed to be an experience for all who wanted to participate—essentially an extension of the physical education experience.

The problems began when the first call was issued for all fifth and sixth grade boys to come out for the track team. Lee, with all his enthusiasm and excitement, showed up with the dream of following in his brother's footsteps and being the star sprinter. He signed up for virtually all the events, except of course those that no one wanted to do, like throwing the shot and participating in the longer runs.

His first race against other competitors ended up much like the race portrayed on the Andy Griffith show where Opie runs in the sprint race for the town of Mayberry. For anyone who has not seen the episode, Opie trains hard with Barney and has convinced himself he will be the fastest and will win the race. The gun fires, the runners take off and it is quickly apparent that Opie will not win. As a matter of fact, Opie ends the race in last place. So it was with Lee.

With his dream of star sprinter behind him and now not knowing what else to do, Lee walked to the shot-put area and began to throw the shot, knowing that at least he could be on the team by participating in this event. This is where bad went to worse, and Lee was not able to compete there as well. The teacher—instead of being understanding, caring and nurturing—ridiculed, laughed and told Lee to go home because he was too weak to even throw the shot for the team. Please don't misunderstand and think I believe every child can or should be on the team. It was not what the teacher/coach did; it was the way he did it.

To say Lee was devastated was, to my understanding, an understatement. Even after two years to heal, Lee was still noticeably hurt as he told the story. If only someone could have cared and understood, the suffering could have been lessened for the boy. Not only did the coach jump in on the laughter, but because he did, the other boys did as well, and Lee picked up his first new nickname, Sow. At the time young Lee didn't understand and thought the boys were saying "Sal," something completely different. It wasn't until later he understood they were commenting on his size and the nickname was not one of friendship but of mockery.

Here is a prime example how a teacher can destroy a child with words and deeds. Others outside of education can do the same thing, as did the person at church Lee mentioned earlier. When dealing with children, Lee taught me it is so important to measure our words and actions. Something that may seem funny or easy to joke about with a young child may hurt them deeper than we could ever know. Our job in society is to build up our children, not tear them apart.

The next year with his sixth grade teacher, Mrs. Canada, was a much different experience. Maybe it was because Lee's memories were much closer to the time we met, or maybe it was in fact that Mrs. Canada was so special, but whatever the case Lee seemed to perk up when he began to talk about his most recent experiences in sixth grade.

Although Lee shared several things about this most favorite teacher, there were two specific events that showed why this person was a treasure for school children and why I wanted all my fellow educators, including myself, to be just like her. The first characteristic was her ability to observe, know and care for her students. What Lee described may have sounded like no big deal to many, but to Lee it was a life-altering event.

During lunchtime the upper classes were allowed to sell different items to make money for their school proms. One such item was Popsicles. Lee, coming from the poor situation he did, never had the money to purchase one of the delicious treats. Sometimes he said he would swallow his pride and ask one of his friends for money or for them to simply share the treasure with him. On rare occasions they would and, by doing so, would endear themselves to this boy forever.

On one occasion Lee had embarrassed himself and asked for charity from one whom he thought was his friend, and was loudly rejected. The boy had evidently wanted to let everyone know that Lee couldn't even afford the cheap Popsicle that everyone else seemed to have on that particular day. Mrs. Canada observed what happened, and without bringing any more unwanted attention to the young, embarrassed Lee who had separated himself into a corner, she quietly and with no one else knowing gave this "throwaway" kid the money to purchase the treat. As you would expect, Lee tried to turn her down and say it was okay, but she would hear nothing of it and saw to it that he was served. You see, Mrs. Canada cared about more than just what Lee was learning academically and wanted him to know people cared about who he was. Wow, I wanted to be just like Mrs. Canada!

Another life-changing experience that year was sparked by Mrs. Canada and her joy of reading. Lee's home was basically void of books, and no one really ever read in front of him or to him. He said the only time he could remember seeing his father read was in bed on Sundays and reading the paper. Mrs. Canada, on the other hand, modeled to the students the joy and excitement they could gain through reading. To do this she would take time each day, usually right after the noon recess, and sit with the children and read aloud to them. Not just a short story or poem (although I understand she did this as well), but an entire book. Each day Lee said he would be so excited to see what was going to happen in the book. With excitement in his eyes and passion in his voice, he began to tell me how the story would come alive as Mrs. Canada read. When I asked him what book she read last year he said with a smile, *"White Fang."*

Later in life Lee told me that Mrs. Canada's read-alouds caused him to be turned on to reading and, from that point on, in his education and personal life he became an avid reader. Having never known how an author could bring vivid images into the mind through words, Lee had depended on his friend, the television, for all his images. Until Mrs. Canada introduced to him the world in his mind, he had been trapped in the world of the television. Isn't it a tragedy today that we have fewer and fewer parents and teachers like Mrs. Canada who understand the power of the written word? Wouldn't it be wonderful if instead of worrying totally about standards and testing adults could take more time to sit, read and share with the young people in our homes and our schools?

In my mind I reexamined my own teaching methods and my attitude toward students as I listened to Lee's story. Was I too focused on test scores and not enough holistically on each child as an individual? I yearned to know what each student wanted and needed to bring out his or her best. I began to brainstorm new ways, like Mrs. Canada's passion for sharing books, that I could expand a child's mind and horizons simply by showing them something new, or sharing a passion of my own that could somehow inspire them.

The Middle School Years

LEE'S MIDDLE SCHOOL YEARS, grades six through eight, were much like his peers'. He was trying to understand how he was changing and growing both physically and emotionally. It seemed that all the stress he was going through with the issues with his father and seeming lack of love and support at home only made this life transition period even more difficult for him.

Toward the end of the first year of our relationship, I began to notice a profound difference in Lee and his attitude toward life. This once joyous young man, even in his circumstances, began to be more withdrawn and pitiful. His weight became more and more of an issue as he got larger and larger. He began to miss school, and when he did come and we had our meetings together, I could hardly get him to talk. His grades, although still better than average, tailed off a bit, mainly because of his excessive absences.

I finally felt it necessary to contact his home to see if I could get to the bottom of this dramatic change in his behavior. His family had noticed him being despondent, but had chalked it up to just being a kid and really had not thought it to be much of a problem. When asked about the absences, Lee's mother realized he was missing more than normal, but she was busy working and really had no time to argue with him in the mornings about going to school and was many times gone before it was time for Lee to get on the bus. She therefore didn't know that he had stayed home until she got home from work.

Something had to be done as I saw myself losing Lee and he had surely lost his joy. I tried to no avail to get him to open up and let me inside his head to see what was bothering him enough to make him so sad. I called his mother again and asked what could have happened in Lee's life to cause such a radical change. Finally after many questions, I had a ray of hope into the possible reasons for Lee's spiral downward to depression. Lee had not told me, or any of the staff, of his recent loss of his grandfather on his father's side. I decided to talk to Lee again to see if that could be any part of the problem.

The next day I met with Lee, and I had no reason to believe I would learn the depth of knowledge that I did. After this meeting I learned many young people go through exactly what Lee was going through. This enabled me to help several children through the rest of my career in education. You see, the death of Lee's grandfather was what caused the beginning of Lee's problem. It was, however, not the loss of his grandfather that caused his depression, but rather the overwhelming realization that seeing his grandfather in the coffin had caused in Lee—he suddenly came face to face with the fact that he would someday die and be placed in a coffin as well. This realization of his own mortality had paralyzed this young man to a place where he was, in fact, becoming physically ill thinking about his own death. It was so consuming that he could not function normally. His mother, father and other teachers had noticed his state but did not take the time to uncover the cause of his situation. They concluded that it was just a phase he was going through and it would soon pass.

I would like to tell you that he immediately got over his fear of death, but that was not the case. Once we talked, however, and he admitted out loud to someone what the problem was, we were able to spend our next few times together discussing it. He came to the understanding that his thoughts and feelings were not abnormal at all, but his letting it have such a profound effect on his life was something he could not continue to allow to happen. This took us some time, but Lee overcame this struggle and came back to being his normal self. Yet another problem lingered — there was even more of him than there was before he went through this emotional distress. His time at home and his state of depression had caused his overeating to go into warp speed.

19

Weighty Issues

URING THESE MIDDLE SCHOOL YEARS Lee's weight was the most out of control that it ever was. The issues of his father's alcoholism, his struggle with mortality, his poverty and general lack of joy in life all helped cause him to find more and more comfort in food. He would eat to feel good and then feel horrible that he was getting larger and larger, so he would eat more to feel better, and this unhealthy cycle of eating just got worse and worse.

As a teacher and person who cared about this child, I tried without much success to help Lee through this weight gain. He would come into our sessions and more and more his time was spent expressing his despair of not being able to control his life and his weight. One particular session illustrates an example of what Lee was experiencing:

I had a really bad weekend. You know we had that class party this weekend at school? Well, I thought it was going to be great. I found this red sweatshirt that I could wear on the outside of my pants that I thought covered up my fat pretty well. I just knew I could go and have fun like all the others, and maybe even Jane would notice me. You know I have always wanted to be Jane's boyfriend since I was in second grade. Well, the evening started out okay, and I had a chance to be with Jane and her friends for awhile. Then we played basketball, and I started sweating, and my sweatshirt got all wet and sticky, and my fat kept showing more and more. I was embarrassed and went off by myself. I knew as soon as I got to school on Monday that I would be made fun of. That didn't happen, but Jane hasn't talked to me at all. I think at times I would just be better off not being here at all.

How sad that this boy with such promise was so dejected and defeated. I began talking to him about what he had going on that was positive to try and get him out of his mood. He was playing basketball, and his team was having more success than any other middle school team had ever had. He did seem to cheer up a bit as he thought and talked about his team, but that particular meeting ended up with these words:

Thanks for listening to me and helping, but being so fat is awful. I can't even tuck in my basketball shirt because my fat shows so much. I just wish I could make all the fat disappear. I try and hide over in a corner when I dress for practice and games so the other guys won't look at me. Why can't I be like all the other guys?

The Transformation Begins
As I stated earlier, Lee had told me that he was not going to end

up like his dad. He had made this pledge just before we met, and soon after the discussion of his weight I began to notice the first of several positive changes in Lee. His grades began to consistently improve. His weight was most certainly still an issue, but he began to take great pride to let me know his grades were on the rise and his goal was to be one of the very best students in his class. It seemed that even though he couldn't fit in physically with the other students, he found he could be their equal or better when it came to academics and, surprising enough, he gained equality on the basketball court, even with the excess weight. Both these successes seemed to bolster his desire to continue to improve and escape the bonds of his personal problems.

Our meetings seemed to be more and more sporadic, many times triggered by some event or issue that Lee would have in trying to cope with the changes going on in his emotions and his body. His weight issues became the worst during his eighth grade year. What specifically was going on I can only speculate, but I do know his father's drinking seemed to peak during this time. To explain how out of control Lee's weight became, all one has to do is examine the eighth grade basketball program. Lee was playing guard on a very successful team that went undefeated until the last game of their tournament where they were defeated by one point. Lee was listed at 5' 6" tall and 169 pounds, clearly much heavier than the rest of his teammates.

During one summer the toll from catching all the baseball games for all those formative years finally caught up with Lee physically. As he had told us earlier, he had filled the position of catcher on all his teams since he was seven years old. The tendon in his right knee had begun to pull from the bone and he had to be put in a cast for nearly the entire summer.

During his months in the cast he spent his days in the local

American Legion post with his retired grandfather on his mother's side of the family. Papaw, as Lee referred to his grandfather, spent a great deal of time with this young boy in a cast teaching him to play Snooker, a billiard game requiring a high level of skill and control. Lee was a quick study and was soon beating his grandfather consistently.

On one particular day Papaw had a bit of fun with Lee when the local Snooker shark came into the hall to play. The man asked Papaw to play and Papaw said, "No, why don't you play the kid here?" That was not what the man had in mind, but he did want to play so he "spotted" the kid 20 points on the line. The game was on! By the time the table was clear, Lee had defeated the proud player by 25 points, five more than was originally spotted. Papaw cheerfully collected his bet, and the teacher and his student walked silently away. Because Lee beat one of the best, his reputation as a player quickly spread, and he was no longer given a handicap from any of the regular players.

Just after school started, Lee was out of the cast but still unable to play any sports. It took well into the basketball season of his freshman year for him finally to get back to being physically able to play. During this same period of time Lee also missed several days of school. In fact, he missed two full weeks because of a mild form of scarlet fever. When I checked on his status, I was told he had been running a very high fever and was unable to keep food down for several days.

I know it sounds unbelievable, but when Lee returned after those few weeks, it was as if I had witnessed a transformation before my very eyes. The fever and inability to eat had caused him to lose a significant amount of weight, and his body also chose this very time to give him a growth spurt. The big change happened not just during those two weeks, but throughout the year, and this once short, obese little boy became a slim, tall young man. Lee went from the 5'6" and 169 pound middle-schooler to a 6'1" and 150 pound high school athlete.

Still No Self Esteem

Lee behaved as though all was right with his world, and most of his peers and teachers bought his façade. His grades were excellent, he was thin, he was excelling on the athletic field and he had begun to catch the eyes of some of the young girls. However, when Lee and I sat down to discuss how things were going in his life, it was as if I was talking to the same boy I met those few years before. Lee was still fighting his same issues at home, and his perception of himself had not significantly improved from those early meetings.

Lee said that when he looked at himself in the mirror, he still saw the same little fat body that he had always had. He also felt that people still did not respect him or take him very seriously. When speaking of his relationship with the young girls or with his friends, Lee could not believe anyone telling him that any girls he knew might be interested in him. While many of his friends were beginning to pair up, Lee always found himself the loner at any social activities that his acquaintances participated in. When talking to Lee privately, one could sense the loneliness this young man suffered. It seemed no matter how much talking we did, he could not be convinced he was worthy of male or female friends; even in amiable social situations, he could be alone in a crowd.

Yet when I spoke with his classmates, they would see him in a totally different way. To those around him, Lee was perceived as very self confident and, to some, even a bit overconfident. Wow, was that a tough one! This young man was so out of touch with how he was perceived.

Even after these other conversations, I was really never ever able to get Lee to have what I would call a healthy view of who he was and how he was perceived. Lee constantly struggled and still fights his self image issues today. He also continued to use the same coping mechanisms that he learned early in his life to isolate, insulate and protect himself from the possibility of someone hurting him. Lee then and still is able to be "alone in a crowd." To the outsiders who didn't know Lee the way I did, he appeared to be a well-adjusted, successful young man. Inside, he still hurt and suffered, but not to a point of paralysis. It never took much to take Lee mentally back to his early years and into his feelings of being different and of little worth.

20

The Work of Life Begins

IN ONE OF OUR LAST MEETINGS at the end of Lee's freshman year, he informed me he didn't know how much longer he was going to be able to compete in athletics. He had been able to exist with odd jobs, working for local farmers and the like, but it was time he was going to have to find a more permanent job so he could try and make enough money to carry him through the next school year. He was also going to have to pay for his class ring and other school expenses. It seemed Lee's parents' idea of helping and raising children was a bit different from others. Perhaps because they had very little growing up and lived through hard times, they saw it as the children's responsibility to provide as much as possible for their own care. If Lee or his siblings wanted even some items to take care of their basic needs, they had to provide them. The parents supplied the home and food, but other than that, the responsibility rested on each child.

Shortly after summer began I found that Lee was working in a local drive-in restaurant. In our first meeting at the beginning

of the next school year, Lee poured out his heart and the humiliation he once again had to live through:

Well, I made it through the summer at the job, but it was
tough. It was the only steady job I could find, and so I had
to take it. The good thing is that I was able to save some
money, but it was not much fun. I had to start out with
the lowest position, waiting on customers in their cars. I
didn't make much money and was supposed to make it
up on tips. I was only one of two guys who were given the
job, and the rest were good-looking young girls. You can't
imagine the hassle I got, especially since the other guy was
a bit feminine. Some of the time it wasn't too bad, but
then when some of the older guys who had their licenses
would come in, they would make my life miserable and of
course leave me no money. I'm just glad I got promoted
quickly to a cook and didn't have to suffer the humiliation
any longer.

Lee's sophomore year in high school was much more of the
same; he continued to make good grades and had success on the
athletic fields, but made no progress in a healthier self image. The
success on the basketball floor of Lee and his teammates was
beginning to catch the eye of the community and the local media.
Since their seventh grade year the same group of young men had
only lost four games, and three of those losses were in the first
four games of their seventh grade season. They lost one in the
eighth grade season (the final game of their tourney), and they
were undefeated as freshmen. The sophomore year was more of
the same, and as the high school reserve team they were once
again undefeated. At the same time the varsity team was having

great success as well, and Lee and some of his teammates were dressing for some of the varsity games; when the varsity won their sectional tournament, these players were allowed to be part of the experience.

Win At Sports a Loss at Home

Between freshman and sophomore years, a significant milestone takes place in the lives of most adolescents. They take driver education, and after they have their sixteenth birthday, they get the privilege to drive legally on the road. Of course, with Lee's home life he knew his chances of having something to drive provided by his parents were slim to none, or at least driving anything he wouldn't be ashamed to be seen in. He therefore took it upon himself to save enough money to buy himself a car after working all summer. Lee managed to buy an old, beat up car off one of those roadside lots that specializes in selling cars that have long since seen their useful life. He did find one that had a fairly good engine, but it was very rough on the outside and needed a lot of work to make it satisfactory so that Lee would feel good about being seen in it.

Lee's birthday was in November, so every bit of time he had through the summer he spent lovingly bringing back his prized possession to life, a life Lee could only imagine. He told me how he dreamed of driving to school like many of his friends and being able to drive himself home from his practices rather than having to bum a ride off one of his teammates, to wait for someone to pick him up or even at times to walk the two miles to his home.

That dream of driving his very own new car finally came to fruition—but like so many of his dreams, it was overshadowed by disappointment. Because he did not hold a driver's license yet, he could not drive on the road without an adult and, as fate would have it, that opportunity would cruelly never materialize.

Just before Lee turned 16 and would finally be free to come and go as his beloved car could take him (and as he could afford to put gas in the car), he experienced a disappointment that he only recently was able to let go.

I have to talk to you and get this off my chest. I know you shouldn't be hung up on material things, but the way this happened and the timing was really hard to handle.

As you know, I worked all summer and was able to save some money. I thought I could probably buy an old used car and take the time I had before I turned 16 to fix it up. My dad helped me and we found an old Buick at a used car lot. Dad knew the guy who ran the place and they started haggling over the price. I wanted to just give the guy the money he asked. I had just that amount in my account ... I could already see myself behind the wheel of that car!

My dad, on the other hand, knew the guy and knew he'd built plenty of profit margin into the car to negotiate. I was so scared he was going to walk off without my getting the car, but he was amazing! He talked, negotiated, laughed and finally said what his bottom dollar was going to be. The sales guy said, "No way" and Dad told me to come with him, we were leaving. My heart sank. I tried to argue, but Dad looked at me where the guy couldn't see, winked and started to walk toward our car. We hadn't walked but a few steps when I heard the salesman yelling, "Stop!" We turned, walked back and made the deal for the dollars my dad had offered.

That day had to be one of the best days of my entire

life. I wrote the guy a check from my own checking account and still had money left that I could spend on fixing up the car. That was so special because my dad and I had a great time. We came back later with Mom and picked up the car, and of course Dad drove it home. I don't know why I didn't because I had my permit, but I think Dad was as excited as I was that he had made a great deal.

I have been working on my car almost every day. I actually spray-painted the outside a hideous green. I can't say it was a great paint job, but it's okay. The only thing I have been able to do is start the car and drive back and forth in the yard. It was a straight stick, so I never got it out of first gear, but at least I was still driving.

I actually named the car. I think I told you before but my nickname is Sal. I named my car Sal's Cyclone. It may sound lame, but I like it. (Lee was unaware the kids were really calling him Sow).

You are not going to believe what happened! The other day when I came home after basketball practice, I couldn't wait to look out back to check out the Cyclone. To my surprise, it was not there. I was panicking inside … where the heck was my car? I asked Mom where it was, and she very casually said, "Oh, your dad took it up town and put it on a punch board."

(Authors note: In that time, before the advent of the lottery, people gambled many ways. One way was to have this early version of a scratch-off, but it was a card with small holes that had numbers on them. A person would buy chances to punch out one of the numbers and if it was the correct one, they won whatever the prize was, but not until after all of the punches had been sold. The main prize in this instance was Lee's beloved car, which his father had taken without Lee's knowledge. This punchboard raffle allowed Lee's dad to guarantee more money in his pocket than the car was worth.)

When it finally sank in as to what she was saying, I was so shocked I could hardly even speak. When I asked her the question why?, her response was unbelievable. She said, "Well, we have been giving you lunch money for school so we thought you owed it to us." They could have given me lunch money until I graduated and it still wouldn't be what my car was worth. You know my dad used the money for booze.

The Buick Comes Home

Thankfully, there is another story attached to this unpleasant memory from Lee that somewhat atones for his devastating experience. Recently I had the chance to sit and talk with him and see how God can bring events full circle at a later time to help heal old wounds. Those open wounds he lived with so many years are now just scars that will continue to slowly fade.

Lee had shared the story of his beloved Buick with the members of his current family. One of his sons was so touched by the story and the hurt his father had suffered that he spent the weekend on the Internet and found a car that fit the exact description of his dad's first car. He showed Lee the site he found and they called, set an appointment and went to see the car. His sons bought it and hauled it home.

Lee now finally owns not his original, but a carbon copy of his first car—his beloved Cyclone that his father so callously stole from him. When his sons unloaded the car off the flatbed truck,

Lee got in, started the car up and drove it on the road. This simple act of driving his car down the road was a very emotional event for Lee, for it was the very first time he had driven a car like his own on an actual road. You see, he had never gotten to drive his original Cyclone anywhere beyond the confines of his own yard. Lee's son told me his father's eyes were moist when he pulled back in the drive. His son didn't even realize until that time how meaningful it was for Lee to drive on an actual road. The tears were tears of joy and also a sign of washing away of the bitterness he had held within him for those many years. That cleansing of his eyes was only the beginning of the cleansing that still needs to take place in Lee's life.

21

The Surface Transformation Continues

LEE'S SOPHOMORE YEAR in high school was a time when our friendship seemed to really solidify. Instead of my having to call Lee into an office and pull things out of him, I found him at the door of my classroom often just wanting to talk. This now thin, strong young man was still coming in and sharing from the perspective of the pudgy little sixth grader. As an educator it was eye-opening to continue to observe how others held perceptions of him that were so opposite of what was really going on in the mind and soul of this person.

His friends and teachers saw, I believe, the physical and academic sides of Lee but never could see the emotional side. This was not always their fault as he had become a master of illusion and hid his real self from everyone but me. He also became slightly aggressive and sarcastic on the surface, but I am convinced this was to mask his insecurity and lack of self worth. For all practical purposes, Lee seemed to have it all together. When he would come to me, however, all the pieces of this jigsaw life would come apart and we would attempt together to put them back in place.

During this year, Lee gave me much insight into what I had to do in my career as an educator. He showed me that the way I had made simplistic judgments on children in the past was flawed; I had unwittingly been helping shove children through those cracks in the school system rather than trying to save them from falling through. He made me realize that rather than just reacting to the actions or inactions of young people (and adults as well), that I should try to spend the time finding out why they acted the way they did rather than just responding to the outcomes.

By watching Lee, I know some around him thought of him as conceited and overbearing. As the reader you may find this hard to understand, but Lee had grown out of his fat body and his poverty persona into a seemingly "normal," even aloof, teenager. I knew that his appearance of being aloof came from his early years of making himself alone even in a crowd. Lee had allowed me into his inner circle of feelings but no one else because he didn't want to be hurt even more than he had already been in his short life. Now that his extra weight was gone and he was successful in academics as well as athletics, he was using his satirical manner and his brash personality to keep people from getting too close to him so they couldn't hurt him. I believe Lee has overcome some of this, but he would still tell you that most times he remains alone in a crowd.

There were many highlights in his tenth grade year that would make one think that any problems Lee had in life before then were long gone. He had his first real girlfriend, got his driver's license, went to the regional basketball tournament, kept his weight off, made straight A's in his classes, and was inducted into the National Honor Society—and even ran for office. What a year the young man had! That is what the perception was, but listen to the words of this still introverted, insecure 16-year-old tell about the same events as his sophomore year came to a close:

> *Well, another year coming to an end. Only two more and hopefully I can get away. I don't know how, but I really want to go to college. The problem is I don't know how I can get the money or even how to start trying.*
>
> *I have to go back and work at the drive-in again this year. It is the only job I could find, and I have to get enough money saved to get through next year.*
>
> *Winning the sectional and going to the regional was a blast, but man it was tough not being able to do the things the other guys did. I hadn't been able to work much and I didn't have money. Paul helped me out some, but I hate to mooch off my best friend. He and the rest of the guys are running track now, but since that fifth grade deal I told you about, I hate the sport, and so I am kind of out of the loop now since all my friends are on the track team. I hang out in the gym some and shoot hoops, but they pile it on that I am not out with them. If I thought I could do anything and not embarrass myself I would, just to be around them, but I know I would just end up failing, so why try?*
>
> *I know you know I have been going out with Peggy, but I have to break that off. I realize I was just going with her because she showed some interest, and her being a senior next year and me just a junior, I know it is time to move on. I really don't know how to do it, but I will figure it out somehow.*
>
> *The Honor Society thing was great this year. Something I worked hard for finally happened. Jamie beat me in the elections though. He is a great guy and deserves the office. I know many of those kids don't like me so they*

voted for Jamie. That's okay though because he will do a great job.

I have heard it said and said it many times myself that a person's perception is their reality even though it may be far from the truth. This statement is exactly where Lee was at this time in his life. His image of himself and the image others had of him were vastly different. Others saw him as confident and egotistical, and he saw himself as unworthy and introverted with no self-confidence at all.

How many times do we rush to judgment on people we meet or deal with on a daily basis without really knowing their innermost feelings and conflicts? Lee was teaching me then and has continued to teach me throughout his life what it means to really get to know someone—to know not just how they act and react, but know the why behind those actions. It many times has helped me through the years to be much more understanding of individuals and groups that I would have had very little patience with before the lessons of Lee.

22

Significant Events and Meeting the Significant Other

WHEN LEE RETURNED BACK TO SCHOOL for his junior year, he had continued to grow and mature. He had worked hard all summer to try and prepare himself financially for the upcoming school year so he could continue to play basketball and baseball. In our first visit the first week of school, Lee shared a story of how an individual in his life who had been making a difference for several years, his coach, did so again over the summer. Lee had planned his work week so he could be at the open gym on Monday nights to play basketball and commensurate with his friends—something he couldn't do on the weekends because he was always working. He was also aware that if he didn't show up on those nights, his chances of playing on the varsity squad the next year would be diminished.

Lee was there faithfully every Monday and had begun to hone his skills at a new level. Coaches and players alike were recognizing that Lee had a real chance to gain a starting spot over some of the senior players who would be returning from the very good team of the year before who had gone to the final game of the regional tournament. Of course, because Lee was trying to save every dollar he could, his basketball shoes from the previous season had really outlived their usefulness. While most all of the other players were sporting their new summer purchased shoes, Lee was still in his leftovers from the year before.

On one particular evening Lee experienced what true caring and compassion for others meant. It was an event he shared with me that had a huge impact on his life and has also deeply affected me and my family as well. It was a lesson that I wish more teachers and coaches and people in general could learn from. I will let Lee share the story:

Coach Myer really got to me this summer. He showed me what a great man he is other than just being a great coach. I thought he cared about me more than just as a ball player, but now I know that is the case. One night at open gym we had just finished a pick-up game and were all taking a water break. As was normal, I was kind of off by myself. Coach walked up to me and quietly asked me if I needed some new shoes. I immediately dropped my head at first, not knowing how to respond. I basically whispered, "Yes," and he had that great, kind smile of his and said, "Go up to Modern Sporting Goods and talk to Whitmer. I called him, and he knows you are coming to get the shoes." You know, I know Coach bought those shoes out of his own pocket. Isn't it great that he thought enough of me and cared about me enough to do that? I won't ever forget that act of kindness, and if I ever get the chance, I will do the same for others as Coach has done for me.

I know Lee has been able over the years to do just what he said he would do, sharing what he and his family have with others who are less fortunate. He has also tried to do it in the same manner as Coach—quietly, without fanfare and without embarrassing the one in need. Our family has likewise been touched by this act of kindness and has also tried to model the mindset of Coach and look for ways to help others.

I know it was not why the coach in this case did his act of kindness, but the result was that Lee worked even harder through the rest of the summer and into the fall to make himself the very best basketball player he could be. In fact, the next basketball season Lee did, in fact, along with his best friend Paul, beat out two returning seniors and started all but the first game of the entire season.

Another and more important event happened in Lee's life that summer—an event that would have lifelong ramifications— even though neither he nor I understood it at the time. Lee was working at his job as a cook at the drive-in, and he had severed his relationship with his first girlfriend. One of the activities that made the job bearable was that Lee and his friend Tom would spend time looking out the glass that surrounded them at their grill and fryers in search of girls to flirt with. On one particular night Lee spotted a beautiful young girl . She had long hair and wore very distinctive glasses. This girl luckily left her car and came to the juke box to play a song, so he looked where she was parked and wrote her a note asking her for her name and phone number. She replied and said she would be going out of town with her parents for two weeks, but that he could call her when she returned.

That two weeks passed without Lee thinking much about it, but then he and his friend Paul were out driving one night, and

Lee saw the girl and a friend driving around as well.

I met a great girl this summer! She is not like anyone I have ever met. I thought at first she was Tommy's girl-friend from North Salem, but when I got a chance to talk to her I knew it wasn't Tommy's girl. I started flirting with her at the drive-in and then Paul and I ran into her and her friend. We set a date and we decided to double date ... me with Ann and Paul with her friend. Wow, I never would have thought any girl like her would have ever been interested in me. She is pretty, smart, talented and fun to be with. I only get to see her once a week, but we have a great time together.

I have to tell you though, the first date was a real experience. I thought she was probably rich the way she dressed and acted, so I was really afraid to see where she lived and meet her parents that first night. I could just see my chances of seeing her for any length of time vanish when she would have to see where I lived. To my surprise, when I finally found her house, it was very much ordinary. It was out in the country and not fancy at all. I was even more shocked when I got to the door to pick her up and her dad met me at the door with no shirt on and his boxers pulled up above his shorts he had on. He gruffly greeted me and frankly scared me to death. I did get to know him over the summer though, and he is a great guy and such a kidder that he had greeted me that way on purpose to give me a scare. You can tell he has a special love for his daughter, and he was going to give me a test before he ever let her leave with me.

Paul went out with Ann's friend, and we went to the

show, and I had a great time. Paul and the friend didn't hit it off though, but Ann and I connected, and we have been going out all summer. She and her family are very church oriented, and she is challenging me to get involved in a church more than I am. I really think that I will, because I don't want to lose this girl.

At the beginning of Lee's junior year, anyone who watched him and saw him at school would think he had it all under control and was from an upper or middle class home. Of course all that was not true. He still had to provide for himself and even continued to work at part-time jobs during the school year. Lee still struggled with his insecurities that were entrenched in him and still overcompensated for all his perceived weaknesses. He was still teaching me by his actions how I could help him and others in the future—help them by understanding them and listening to them and giving them a safe refuge to come and be vulnerable and share their deepest feelings. Anyone other than me probably saw Lee as getting more and more brash, self-confident and, at times, sarcastic, but I knew this was all to mask his true feelings of inferiority and fear of failure and being rejected. By his appearing to be "stand-offish" he could remain alone in the crowd and not fear being hurt.

Smoothing the Stone

I was talking with my friends Alecia and Phil the other night at dinner, and I had shared much of Lee's story with them. Alecia gave me a great insight and way to describe Lee and his life. She said Lee was like a piece of marble that had been shaped early in life into his inner form, and every day of his life has been sandblasting the rough spots off the original form. Even though the outer edges seem to become smoother, the interior of the form is still much the same, and it is still flawed.

Academically Lee continued to do better and better. In our conversations over the years, one thing I had been able to get him to understand was that to get himself out of his current environment, he needed to get an education. Even though his family did not have a history of higher education, Lee understood that was his ticket out of his circumstances. He was also very fortunate to have quality teachers in each of his core subject areas, especially in math and English. One of his English teachers, Mrs. Clifton, in his junior English class announced there was a national poetry contest, and if a poem was selected, it could possibly be published. Mrs. Clifton encouraged all to submit a poem but took the time personally to encourage Lee.

Understand that Lee was trying to create and live a macho image of the athletic, self-confident young high school junior. He really hadn't shared much with anyone about his love for reading and writing because again he thought that might give his peers a sense of weakness they could attack, and he would end up hurt. He had shared this love with me and I, too, encouraged him to follow up with Mrs. Clifton's request. Finally, Lee did write a poem in study hall and he quietly submitted it. To his surprise a few weeks later, Mrs. Clifton proudly announced for all to hear that his poem had won and was selected for publication in the National Anthology of High School Poetry. Here is Lee's winning poem. I can see the dark side of Lee's life shows a bit in this first literary attempt.

The End
As I look out among the clouds
I think of days gone by.
I also think of the day to come,
The day I am to die.

What will it say upon the stone
The one at the head of my grave
Will it tell of all my cowardly deeds
Or of my ability to be brave?

One knows nothing about what people think
About them when they are gone.
But I will know of their every thought;
I must die before the dawn.

One cowardly deed on a cold March night
Was enough to end all hope.
I stabbed a man in the back
And now The End comes on the rope.

To Lee's surprise, and mine as well, the news was not only accepted in a positive way by his peers, but it seemed to elevate his standing in the class to a whole new level. Now Lee had achieved something on his own that no one else had been able to do, and his foray into the art of poetry was looked upon as a real positive. It also gave Lee new energy to concentrate even more on his academic success, and through his junior year his grades continued to be stronger and stronger.

Ann's Influence

During his junior year Lee's relationship with Ann continued and seemed to develop into something quite special. I had the opportunity to meet Ann at one of Lee's basketball games, and I could quickly see why Lee was so taken by her. She was a lovely young girl with a beaming smile, and it did not take long to see that she cared deeply for Lee as well. I found that Ann was active in the county with Christian organizations, and I could readily see why Lee was feeling the pressure to get into a church. This was refreshing to me because my wife and I had tried to do the same, but for some reason Ann was having much more of an effect than us.

Lee started attending the church just across the street from his house, and he went faithfully. I asked him once, "Why the quick change?" and he readily admitted that every week when he got the chance to talk to Ann, the first question she asked him was, "Did you go to church?" He didn't want to say no, so he made sure he was there. One would think this type of accountability would be too much pressure, but it didn't appear to be for Lee. Even though he had not made a commitment to Christ at this point in his life, Ann and her family's example began to move him toward that decision.

Wouldn't it be great if more and more young couples started out asking this same question, "Did you go to church?" rather than asking what movie or television show they had watched?

Since Lee did not have many positive experiences in church to this point in his life, he still had questions and was sometimes very uncomfortable. It also didn't help that he always attended by himself with no support from any of his family. After one especially difficult Sunday Lee came to my classroom for counsel on something he had heard in church that really bothered him:

> *You go to church and are a Christian. I need you to ex-*
> *plain something to me. Yesterday in church my Sunday*
> *school teacher told me that hell would be full of a lot of*
> *good people. That really upset me. I know that you know*
> *I have some troubles with my dad, but he is still a good*
> *person as is my mom, brother and sister. You mean to tell*
> *me that God will put them in hell just because they don't*
> *believe in Christ?*

As a public school employee my first reaction was, "Oh no, I can't talk about my faith in this school." After some reflection though, I went ahead and answered Lee by telling him my belief was that no man could ever say who was or was not going to end up in hell. But, the Bible is very clear that if there is not a commitment to believe that Jesus is the one true way into Heaven, that his teacher was right—just living a good life on earth is not a "get in free" card to Heaven. One could lead a respectable, good life and do good things on earth and still spend eternity in hell. After much discussion back and forth, Lee left with a better understanding of what his teacher was trying to convey. Not to say that there was a huge breakthrough at this point in Lee's walk with God, but he was farther down the path than before our talk.

Again Lee taught me a valuable lesson through this experience. Although we must be mindful of the law and follow it, we also need to be ready to speak the truth as we know and understand it and answer questions as forthright as possible. I could have dodged the question, sent him away and left him even more confused, or simply share what I believed. I did not and still don't believe anyone in a public school setting should try to persuade a child to believe in a certain way; I just shared my personal feeling without judging or forcing my beliefs on him. I also suggested he talk to his pastor, teacher, Ann and her parents and they could also help him with his questions. I found out later he did just that.

One final event that seems important to share occurred in the spring of his junior year. As you remember, Lee had a very unpleasant experience with track in his fifth grade year when he was cut from the track team by an uncaring, uncompassionate coach. Since then, Lee had stayed as far away from track as he possibly could. Even though his friends and fellow athletes were involved and his basketball coach also happened to be the track coach, Lee wanted no part of the sport. That was until one day after school:

You are not going to believe what happened yesterday. I was in the gym playing ball after school, and the guys were getting ready for track practice. You know, Paul is the leading sprinter on the team. Well, he was giving me a hard time about how fast he was and how he could beat me in the 100. I knew he probably could too, but he made me mad by just continuing to tease me in front of everybody and giving me a hard time about not being on the team. He finally made me so mad that I bet him I could beat him. He took the bet and outside we went to run before they started practice. Well, there is good news and bad news. The good news is that I beat him. Can you believe it? The bad news is that Coach saw the race, and when we came in he met me at the top of the stairs and told me he would see me at track practice tomorrow. I said, "No way," and he asked if I planned to play basketball next

*year, and I said, "Yes." He then said with that smile of his,
"Then I'll see you at track practice tomorrow." Can you
believe it? The guy that gets cut from the fifth grade team
gets forced to join the varsity? I can't believe it.*

The rest of the story goes like this: Not only did Lee join the
team, but he was immediately the number one sprinter. Ironi-
cally, he broke the school record for the 100 that his brother had
held for several years. I can't tell you that Lee was happy running track, but he was successful, and the team benefited from
his being there.

How different the situation might have been had that track
coach back in fifth grade not discouraged Lee. I thought about the
different course Lee's life might have taken had that coach realized what a difference a kind word could mean to a young boy.
Lee had perhaps missed out on years of involvement in sports,
involvement that would have helped bolster his self confidence
and could have meant success and friendships and joy. In this sce-
nario, it saddened me to think about what Lee had lost through
hurt, years that he would never recover or get a chance to do
over. I strengthened my resolve to always measure my words as
they had the power to kill or to bring life.

Those Remaining High School Years

THE LAST TWO YEARS of Lee's high school career found him going through many of the same issues that others of this age do. His continued to prosper in the classroom, and he continued to move up the scale as far as his academic standing in his class. His athletic career also continued to show promise, and he was a three-sport athlete through his junior and senior years, participating in baseball, track and his beloved basketball. His relationship with Ann continued to grow with the usual bumps one would expect with two high school sweethearts, especially those who don't go to the same school and see each other only on weekends.

Through the summers Lee continued to work for farmers and at the restaurant, and then he landed a job in a gas station. That was a seven night a week job in the summer between his junior and senior year, so there were some troubled times when he worked every night and couldn't even go out on dates with Ann on the weekends. He also had a tough time getting to open gym and oftentimes had to switch hours or lose money to show up.

Again, those on the outside of Lee's circle of confidants only saw him as the All American boy with a beautiful girlfriend, a steady job, athletic talent and academic success. The problem, however, was that Lee's inner circle was not getting larger but was growing smaller and smaller. He continued to withdraw into himself at home, and at school his brash, sarcastic and egotistical behavior drove people away rather than bringing them into his confidence. From my perspective, it seemed his behavior served to distance people from what Lee was really living through so he wouldn't be embarrassed or hurt by the way people would react.

Lee found himself more and more on the outside of social events and parties, looking in rather than being invited to participate. There were several reasons for this, of course, but Lee convinced himself it was because people looked down on him for where he lived and his family rather than the real reason: most knew he worked and couldn't participate if invited. Even though Lee had completely changed in many ways, he still saw himself as the fat, throwaway kid he was in the fifth grade when he was made fun of by both children and adults. Sandblasting had happened on the outside, but the inside remained rough and tarnished.

His home life did not improve. He had little support from home financially or emotionally. This too was of interest to me as a teacher. It was possible that his mother and father really did care for and love him, but they missed the reality of what was going on inside this young man who had it all together on the outside. The sad commentary on the lack of communication between parent and child was that neither understood how the other felt.

What Lee and his family have taught me through this experience, especially as he got older, is how important it is for families to talk—not talk *at* each other, but *to* each other. What I found in Lee's family and others I have subsequently examined is that there are often a lot of words thrown about between child and parent, but many times both parties do not listen. To communicate there has to be a speaker and a listener, but not two speakers. When both parties work so hard to talk, there is not the desire to listen to what the other is saying. Things might have been different had Lee taken the chance to open up to his parents and let them know how much he hurt inside rather than putting on the fake armor of ego that helped deflect anyone who tried to get close to him. Likewise if his mother and father would have known how to initiate real communication and taken the time to actually listen to Lee, they may have been able to help him understand his worth much sooner than he finally did.

One might ask if there was any reason to believe that either side tried to open up the line of communication. From my interaction and observation, there was no evidence that Lee or his family members ever tried actively to make things better. Lee did nothing to give his parents any idea how he hurt, and his parents did little to let him know they loved and cared for him. It seems both just assumed this communication should somehow magically take place.

Events continued to bring Lee into my classroom to unload, and I tried to keep him upbeat and positive about his chances to overcome his situation. One such time was the Monday after the junior prom. Lee came to me as depressed as I had seen him for awhile, and it was evident the prom had not been the joyful experience that he had anticipated. Lee had convinced his father to let him drive the family car to the prom. Even though it was an older car, Lee had cleaned, polished and spruced it up, so he was very proud to pick up Ann for their big date. Of course, Lee was not in a tux or even a suit. He sported hand-me-down clothes that had actually been worn by his older brother eight years ago—at his wedding.

Lee still had high hopes of his evening with Ann as one they both could remember. It was memorable, indeed—but for different reasons. They made it to the prom and had a reasonably good time. After leaving the prom and going to Ann's house to change for after-prom activities, Lee's father's beloved car chose this time to drop a power steering pulley into the fan and subsequently into the radiator. Lee didn't do anything to cause the problem—it just happened—but that is not what Lee's father thought when Lee called his dad for assistance. He and his date finally got home with the gracious help of Ann's family.

As Lee relates this experience, I hope readers will think about how they have been treated or how they have treated their own children or others when something unforeseen happens. Do you think about how your reaction affects the one who receives the brunt of your response? Do you consider the long term ramifications of a short term emotional reaction to an unpleasant accident?

Why do these things always seem to happen to me? I thought Ann and I could have a great time at the prom, and it ended up being another embarrassing and awful night. Embarrassing because we couldn't even finish the prom activities like everyone else because of the lousy car, and awful because of the way my dad responded. When I called him, he acted like I was lying to him and made it clear that I had somehow caused the car to break down. How could someone think that? I told him what happened, and he still yelled at me on the phone for tearing up his car.

*I know he had been drinking, but I still can't under-
stand why he didn't believe me. I have never lied to him,
so it just doesn't make sense. Sometimes it makes me want
to just rebel and be like a lot of the other guys and lie and
cheat and drink and do all sorts of bad stuff just to get
back at him. But then I think that will only hurt me and
not him. I know Ann must think I am a real loser, and
I wouldn't blame her if she just found someone else. She
would be much better off.*

There were several other times those last two years of Lee's
high school career that it was difficult to keep him thinking of
the future and how to change his life rather than succumb to the
environment he was in and just accept the perpetuation of the
lifestyle he had been exposed to throughout his life. Even I had a
tough time understanding at times how he could fight back from
some of the adversity and disappointment that seemed to follow
him.

Strive to Succeed or Fear to Fail?

To relate all the events in Lee's life would not really move his story
of success forward, but generally speaking there were financial,
relational, emotional and athletic challenges he had to overcome
to get closer to breaking the chain of failure that was perpetuated
through most of his life. For a teacher and observer, the paradox
was, however, that if one did not know otherwise, Lee seemed
to just keep succeeding more and more. But the sad fact was that
Lee was being driven to succeed out of an intense fear of failure
rather than an inner drive for success. The result was a driven
person rather than a happy one. Each achievement was tempered
by Lee feeling that he had to strive to accomplish even more to

be accepted or valued.

Of course, when looking at Lee's relationship (or lack of) with his father, it becomes more understandable as to the types of incidents that caused Lee's feeling of never being good enough no matter how much he thrived. One such example occurred during a very successful year in basketball and in one game in particular. Lee was starting point guard on the team, and they were very successful. They were ranked statewide in the top 20, and Lee was the "coach" on the floor. Because of his role on the team, he was always given the toughest defensive assignment and was given the responsibility to initiate and run the offense. This role caused him not to be the one scoring most of the points. In one particular game, however, Lee's offensive skills shined, and he scored 22 points, hitting 11 of 12 field goal attempts and leading his team to victory over a very tough opponent.

The following week, Lee shared with me that he had really never felt as proud of his playing ability as he did that particular night, and he couldn't wait to get home because he just knew he would finally get the recognition from his father for the great offensive game he had. His dad had always commented about all the other players scoring points but had never really seemed to value Lee's contribution to the team. To his surprise, when he began to try to talk to his father about the game, the very first thing his dad said was, "You didn't play much defense tonight."

Please, listen to yourself and think before you talk to your children, young people under your care or simply those you love or come in close contact with. Although Lee's dad probably didn't mean to hurt his child, he did. It was a moment when one affirmative word would have meant the world to Lee. Instead, it served a just another brick in Lee's wall around himself and another self-doubt put into his mind about his skills and abilities.

During Lee's senior year there were many events that continued to move him forward in his quest for normalcy, and then inevitably something would happen to pull him back into the bondage of his past and his environment. During this time his father also had a very serious setback when he was demoted in his job. He had worked for the same company for well over 20 years, and the job he was so good at basically went away. New technology and product improvements made his job obsolete, which meant he got "bumped" back to very menial labor, devastating his already fragile psyche.

Looking back now, it is clear that Lee's father was very much like Lee. After having come to that realization, I did some further checking and found that Lee's father had fought all his life with a low self-esteem and a feeling of not being worthy. He masked this, much like his son, by overcompensating and having a bravado about him that caused those around him to see him as a self confident, self indulging and self centered person. I really believe this pretense, along with his dependence on alcohol, was his way of coping with failure or at least a lack of the achievement he always felt he should have accomplished. The sad thing about Lee's father is that he never understood or came to grips with his problems, and instead of breaking the chain of low self worth, he nearly created another link by the way he treated his son. This made it much harder for Lee to break out of the cycle.

College Dreams, With Harsh Reality

EE'S FATHER EVENTUALLY found a good paying
job in a very profitable company. He had a lot of responsibility and the opportunity to take his family to a whole
different plane as far as a standard of living. This was at the time
Lee was preparing to try to go to college, so it looked like there
might finally be a good break in Lee's life of struggle. Lee had
taken the SAT and had done very well. His scores were some of
the highest in his class, and talking with him you could see that,
where before there was not even a glimmer of hope of going to
college, he now could visualize the dream. Even though there had
never been anyone in Lee's family ever apply for entrance into
college, we were able to get his paperwork completed and the
financial aide forms filled out by his family.

The problem then came when Lee was denied financial aide
because his father and mother now made too much money. Lee
was now left with the entire responsibility on his own because
his mother and father made it plain that they would not help him
since they had not helped their two older children. In their minds

they had convinced themselves it would not be fair, or they just chose not to help. Perhaps they believed that it would mean more to Lee to go on his own rather than helping him, or perhaps they just didn't know how hard it would be.

Lee managed to have his mother write a check for the entrance form fees, and he was accepted into Purdue University. According to Lee, that was in large part the only money his parents provided. At times they would visit and bring food, but they provided no financial support.

His scores would have allowed him to go anywhere he desired, but the dollars were a major stumbling block. The reason he chose Purdue was that, because of his SAT scores, he was offered an alumni scholarship for academics that paid his tuition, without which he could never have attended.

Of course, tuition was only a small part of the overall costs of his education. He still had to come up with room and board as well as pay for his books and fees. Between his senior year of high school and his freshman year at Purdue, he worked and saved enough money to get him through the first semester. In speaking with him and trying to get him to think beyond his freshman year, he could only focus on what he knew he could do, and that was to get through the first semester. I really didn't think, as probably did Lee, that he would ever make it the full four years to earn a bachelor's degree.

During that summer before he entered college, Lee and Ann's relationship kept progressing, and whether out of desperation, love or infatuation, Lee asked Ann to marry him. She accepted, and they planned to marry at the end of his freshman year. I am sure many agreed with my opinion that these two children were a bit crazy to even believe that if they married that finishing school would be a possibility.

To my surprise and everyone else's, the two young people didn't even wait until the end of Lee's freshman year to get married. They stepped up the date and married at the end of his first semester. Although most of their family and friends thought they were just out of their minds, they had carefully thought out their plans, and the major reason for the marriage timing was so that Ann could help Lee stay in school. She had gone through an extensive interview with a company in Lafayette and had been offered a good paying job that would allow Lee to stay in school. All she had left to do after the big wedding day on Sunday was to pass her physical on Monday, and she would start her new job on Tuesday.

In one of our now more infrequent times to talk, Lee had shared that his love for Ann had continued to grow even more since she had decided to sacrifice her academic plans to help him fulfill his dream of attaining a college diploma. Ann was very bright and talented in her own right and could have gone anywhere she chose, but she was determined to help Lee and lay a groundwork for their future. All of that was great and their plans were fine, except:

You are never going to believe what happened. Ann and I got back to our trailer after our wedding and on Monday she went to take her physical and go to work. When I got home from class, she was crying, and we found out she did not pass her physical. She was found to be anemic and had low blood pressure, and the company would not hire her. I didn't know what we were going to do. We had gotten married with the promise of the job and the income from it. We actually had no money in the bank and only one month of our housing paid for. The only food we had was

the food people had given us as wedding presents and the
only money we had were those monetary gifts people had
given us. Those dollars wouldn't even take us through the
next weeks, let alone the next semester.

Lee and his young bride were destitute and had no place to
turn but to one another. Lee did what he had always done and
began to try to find a way to survive. He shared with me that
failure at this point was not an option, and he would not let those
who had prejudged him and his actions be right. He went about
finding a job, and he actually began to work seven days a week
while going to school at the same time. Ann tried to find a job,
but it was much tougher for her, and she needed to take care of
herself physically.

On the surface, Lee and Ann seemed to be making it. Lee
was still in school, Ann was coming back to health, and the two
actually even bought a mobile home. All of this was surface
appearances, but few had the magnifying glass that I did. Lee was
struggling and was going on few hours of sleep. He had to keep
up his grades because if he slipped below the standards set to
keep his scholarship, the dream of a college degree would be lost.
Ann and Lee were surviving, but not living. They had each other,
and that was about it. Again, Lee was able to make himself alone
in a crowd of thousands of students at school and in the crowd of
workers at his factory job, but he never allowed anyone to get a
glimpse of his real feelings. His façade of being all together and in
control was well built, and this wall kept those around him from
penetrating his fears and shortcomings.

Ann finally got healthy and got a pretty good job at a local
drug store, which allowed Lee to take part-time jobs so he could
concentrate more on his school work. The reality is that had it

not been for Ann and her commitment to Lee and his school work, he would never have finished. On one of his trips home he sat with me and shared a specific event that showed Ann's dedication to Lee and his educational journey:

I don't know why I am so blessed to have Ann as my wife. I was getting so discouraged and tired of fighting to get through school that I called my uncle and asked him for a job. He said yes, and I could start at the end of the term. I would only have completed my sophomore year. I was pretty much convinced that was what I was going to do. When Ann got home, I told her what I had done and expected her to be happy that she was going to be able to quit work and we could start our family and stop having to figure out how we were going to make it. Imagine my surprise when she asked, "Is that what you want to do for the rest of your life?" I thought for a moment and had to answer truthfully and say "No," but that was not the point. We could get out of the situation we were in and we could have money. She looked at me and smiled and said to call my uncle back and tell him I was going to stay in school. She is the best! She is willing to sacrifice short term so we can have the life we both believe we want for the future. Not too many people would do what she has done.

Lee was right; Ann was and still is a very special person. Through the college years she did whatever it took to make sure the long term goal of a college education and a "normal" family life would be in place. While many others were trying to form new links in the chain of failure, Ann was helping Lee forge the key of education to help unlock and break the chains already formed.

It was never easy, and Ann and Lee never did things the "typical" way. They decided at the end of his sophomore year that they had waited long enough and they wanted to start their family. Here were two young adults trying to put themselves through school, and they make the decision they want to have children! Of course, that meant that Lee would have to go back in the full-time workforce, but that is a decision they made together and they believed they could pull it off.

Of course, reality finally sunk in after their first baby was born when the expenses of raising a child and trying to go to college at the same time hit like a lightning bolt in a spring storm—and the effects were just about as devastating. Lee had a full-time job, but making just above minimum wage didn't pay for the diapers, formula, doctor and hospital bills that came along with the bundle of joy. But as often happens, Lee and Ann learned valuable lessons during this time of stress and stretch. They learned they had to be a team and sacrifice. Ann quietly, willingly, sacrificially went back to work, first babysitting other married students' children and then back to her former employer at the drug store.

Ann's Family Gift

Another life lesson learned was how to give and how to receive. Ann's parents were not rich people financially, but they were rich in their willingness to give and support. On more than one occasion Lee told me of how Joe and Mary, Ann's parents, came to the aid of the two young impetuous college students and supported them by loaning them money to survive. Lee shared that it was very difficult for him to ask and then accept the money, but he also learned about how to give. Lee shared that each time he and

Ann asked for money, Joe and Mary never asked why or for what the money was needed; they simply gave. Mary would look at Joe and say, "Go write the kids a check," and the only question would be "How much?" The big lesson that Ann and Lee learned came much later in their adult life. I will let Lee share that wonderful lesson in his words:

> *I have got to tell you what happened. As I told you many years ago, Joe and Mary really helped Ann and I get through school by loaning us money on more than one occasion. Through the years we have systematically tried to repay the loans as we could. They have never asked us to have any sort of formal payment schedule. I think they realize that trying to raise a family is expensive, and they just never asked for the money. While we have been able to pay some, we were not close to having what we owed them paid off. The other day we got a card signed by both Joe and Mary. It said, "Your debt has been forgiven." I can't tell you how deeply this touched my heart and Ann's. What a lesson! They just forgave our debt. When and if we ever get into the position to do the same for our children, we will. What a blessing Ann's folks have been in our life, and what a valuable example of what parents should do for their children.*

Ann and Lee made it through those last two years of college to earn his bachelor's degree, but not before they weathered more challenges together. After the first child was born and Lee was working full time, it was discovered that Ann had been injured during the birth and was going to need surgery. The two had bought health insurance for the birth of the baby, but it was nowhere near enough to cover both the birth and then another surgery. The medical bills were mounting as was their stress level. On top of that Lee contracted pneumonia while working with chemicals at his job and ended up in the hospital, unable to work for several weeks. This was one of those times when Ann's family came to the rescue and saved them financially.

Through all of this Lee was able to keep his scholarship and ultimately graduated with honors and received the president's academic award at the end of his senior year. He and Ann had worked together tirelessly to reach the goal of that college degree, doing whatever it took to survive and succeed.

Journey From Being Served to Serving

NOT LONG AGO I was sitting in Orlando at a Disney Resort eating my breakfast. As I was being served by a very pleasant waiter and my every need being met so that my breakfast could be an enjoyable experience, it reminded me of Lee's life and the significant people who had broken through to serve him and give him hope. It occurred to me that now Lee was in a position to return that service so others could find hope as well. It was time for him to get up from the table where he had been fed the valuable lessons of life and be the one serving those who needed it. Lee shared with me this desire to make an impact on others.

To do this, Lee embarked on a career in education. To understand this choice, one need only to look at the people who had the biggest impact on Lee's life—the teachers and coaches who challenged, inspired and disciplined him through his formative years and beyond.

One of those influential educators was Lee's coach for all his competitive years through high school. Upon graduation, Lee had taken a job in a factory and had accepted his first teaching and coaching job at the school where his former coach was employed. The teaching position was satisfactory, but the coaching was not what Lee had hoped for. He wanted to coach with his former mentor; however, the job that was available was not going to allow that to happen. Still, though, Ann and Lee were very happy Lee had his first real job, and they quickly moved into an apartment in the community where Lee would be teaching.

To try to keep food on the table, Lee had accepted a summer factory job where his father worked, and he drove a "mule" (fork lift truck). It was a steady job, and the money was decent. As a matter of fact, it was probably more money on an hourly basis than Lee would be making as a teacher/coach, but it was not what he wanted to do with his life and for the life of his family. He worked the afternoon shift from three in the afternoon to eleven in the evening. Lee did not like the job at all, but as he had done so many times before in his life, he did what he needed to do to survive.

One evening shortly after the two had moved into their apartment, Lee's former coach called Ann and asked her if they had unpacked their boxes from the move. When Ann replied they had not completed the task as yet, the coach replied, "Then don't." Ann didn't know what to think, and Coach said he would be over the next day to explain before Lee went to work. The following day he came to the small apartment and explained that he had been offered a head coaching job in the southern part of the state, and he wanted to take Lee with him as his assistant. This was Lee's dream come true and, of course, he quickly accepted the offer. He would be an English teacher, an assistant basketball coach and, yes, the head track coach. Lee was actually going to head up the sport that had caused him so much pain as a young boy.

Of course, like most other beginning teachers Lee and Ann were still struggling to make it financially. Because the coach knew Lee's situation very well, he took it upon himself to help Lee get a job at the school during the summer months before classes began. This helped pay the rent on Lee and Ann's house and the expenses of moving two and one half hours away. Remember, this was the second move in just a few weeks.

His first job in the school business after receiving his education degree was summer help on the janitorial crew. It was hard, hot and menial work without much glory or fanfare, but work that Lee was used to and completed without complaint. As a matter of fact, it probably started Lee's career better than most because he immediately had empathy for what the custodians had to deal with to maintain a healthy learning environment for children.

My teaching career didn't start off quite like I had expected. Ann and I moved down to our new rental house, and I began the following Monday working under Donnie, the head custodian, getting the schools ready for the upcoming school year. You know I had always thought it crazy that teachers wouldn't allow students to chew gum in school, and as a new teacher I was going to get rid of that stupid rule. That is until I spent my first week on the job scraping gum off the floors of the school and from under desks with a putty knife. After just the first day I made myself a promise that students would NEVER chew gum in my class or school if I could keep them from it. When you get into someone else's shoes, you see why some things are the way they are!

With the summer over and the first day of school quickly approaching, Lee was anxious to begin his career in the profession he loved and respected so much. He was to teach junior high and freshman English and to serve as the homeroom teacher for a group of seventh graders coming into the middle school. It strikes me that seventh grade was the very same time in Lee's life that we first met. I was much like an expectant father waiting and watching as his child is born; I was waiting and watching to see how Lee would handle his career and what kind of influence he would now be on those children under his care. Would he remember the lessons he had been taught and lived through, or would he be like so many of my peers who had become hardened and uncaring, just doing a job rather than having a mission?

I know that many first days on the job are uneventful and forgettable, but Lee's could not be classified in either of these two areas. During his homeroom period, the first task was to fill out enrollment and information cards.

The first day wasn't what I had expected. I was, of course, a bit nervous. Being pretty young and these kids coming into the junior high, I had myself all prepared to be the strong disciplinarian I knew I would have to be. I handed out the information cards and told them to fill them out. Of course, on the first line was NAME. I had no more than got back to my desk, looked around and a rather odd looking, unkempt boy in the very first row had his hand raised. Of course I didn't know their names as yet so I said, "Yes?"

He then said, "How do you make a capital R?"

I just knew I was going to have my first discipline problem on the first day and that would not look good to my new principal. I replied by saying, "Just fill out the card!"

I went on about my business and when I looked up again, the very same student was holding up his hand again! I again answered, "Yes?" but with a bit more bite in my voice.

He then said, "How do you make a capital R?"

I now had to restrain myself from shouting at the young man and making a fool out of myself as I was calculating in my mind how I was going to remove this discipline problem out of my room. About this time, a rather meek looking peer of my problem child quietly said, "He really doesn't know how to make a capital R." So, my reaction was to quickly turn to the board and make a rather oversized R, and I did so with great flare.

This young man's name was Clarence Rikard, and he really didn't know how to spell his own name. He had all kinds of health problems as well as mental issues and really needed a lot of assistance. My first reaction was not a good one, and my first perception of Clarence was not a good one. I learned quickly that he was a child I could really help by understanding and seeing that he learned as much as he possibly could.

On his very first day of his very first class in his very first year of teaching, Lee had already come across a student he could help. Lee also could relate to this child because Clarence was most definitely not like all the others. Remember from our first meeting Lee was not the best dressed or best looking young man in our school, just as Clarence was not the average looking student. Lee was at this first job for three years, and through all those years he and others like him looked after Clarence and saw to it that he had the most "normal" and successful experience in school possible. Clarence was not ever an academically successful student or one of the "normal" children, but he did have a loving, caring environment in which to succeed to his optimal potential.

The sad ending to the Clarence saga, however, is that not all society and those interacting with Clarence after school were the same as those caring educators in his school. At a very young age, Clarence committed suicide. Lee was devastated by this new. Isn't it sad and a reflection on our society that people outside the walls of the school (and even a few inside) could not see the needs this frail child had and help meet those needs? Instead a very fragile creature of God was torn down to a point of desperation where the only way out of his pain he could discover was taking his life. It strikes me that one major difference between Lee and Clarence was that Lee had developed a way to survive—being alone in a crowd—and Clarence never did. Even though this may not be a healthy mechanism it at least allowed Lee to cope with his circumstances. Clarence was threatened by the crowd and could not cope with society and his differences from the norm, where Lee, with the help of many, learned to cope. It was evident that Lee felt a sense of failure by not being able to do more to help Clarence.

Another Chance to Serve

Lee was given another opportunity to serve shortly into his career. This situation was very similar to Lee's own life and gave him the opportunity to help a young person in need. Rick was so much like Lee at his age. To everyone, on the outside Rick was bright, successful and seemed to have it all together. Even Lee did not know what was going on behind the scenes of Rick's life until one evening when he and Ann heard a knock on the door:

I know you know my life's story, and there have been many times where I just didn't understand why I had to go through everything I had to go through. I think now I am beginning to see why and the value of my going through my life the way I have. The other night Ann and I were home watching TV and we heard a knock on our door. When I went to the door, one of my players was standing there, and you could tell he was very upset. I brought him in and asked him what was wrong. I had no idea this kid was living through what he was. I am sure no one else did either. He had just been kicked out of his house. His mother is clinically insane and his father is a chronic alcoholic. Dad was drunk and Mom was home but not functioning, and Rick was the only sane person in his home. Dad had thrown him out in a drunken rage, and Rick had no place to go. I am not sure why he came to us, but I am sure glad he did.

He shared that his dad had lost their car, had spent all their money and there was no money for food. This is a kid that everyone at school thinks has it all together and is doing great! He puts on a great outward show of normalcy, but is living in hell. He stayed with us all night and went home the next morning. He came back later and asked if there was any way we could spare some money so he could by the family some food. You know that Ann and I barely make it ourselves, but we gave him money. So many have sacrificed for us; that was the least we could do for him.

I love to listen to Paul Harvey and his unique show on the radio. I love his "the rest of the story" segments where he finalizes a story with very strange and unique endings. Well, the "rest of the story" for Rick is that while Lee was in graduate school years later, Rick sent Ann and Lee a check paying them back the money they had given him to buy food. Isn't it heartening that in our self-serving society there are still people who care and show that they do, and people who respond to that caring? It was not that Ann and Lee ever thought they would get the money back, or even wanted it back—it was the integrity of the young man who remembered and repaid someone who cared that made this gesture so special.

The First Coaching Experiences

Rick was one of Lee's first players on his first team he coached. Lee was fortunate to be coaching with his mentor in a nice sized school in the southern part of the state. Lee had much success as a player, but that was not to be as a coach. As good a player as Lee was, he was just not very good as a coach. It is not to say he didn't have success, but not nearly at the same level he experienced as a player. As a matter of fact, he lost more games as a coach his first year than he did all the years he played in junior high through high school.

One of the reasons he did not enjoy a great deal of success as a coach may have had something to do with the players he was dealt. That was never more evident than after that first game which they actually won. Lee, being used to winning nearly every game he ever played in, went into his locker room after the victory to find his players celebrating as if they had won the state championship. Surprised and a bit confused with the excessive exuberance, Lee asked his players what was going on. He quickly found out the game was the first they had won in two years. He should have had an indication that it might be tough to continue his winning ways, but Lee had been blessed with so much athletic success in the past that it took most of the losing season for him to finally be convinced.

During this first coaching experience, Lee was able to bond and grow even closer to his first young son, Allen. Allen was just barely three years old, but he already was enamored with sports and the athletes his dad spent time with each day. Allen was much more mature than most three year olds, both physically and emotionally, and was well on his way to becoming a gym rat. He spent so much time in and around the gym that somehow he managed to become a pseudo student manager and would accompany the team at each game and dutifully hand out the water bottles and towels at each break in the action. When once asked what his duties were by one of the fans after one particular game, Allen proudly announced, "My daddy told me to get the towels, sit on the bench and keep my mouth shut!"

Lee and Ann did not have it any financially easier during their first years of marriage than Lee did growing up. They rented a small house in the small town. They had no money to buy furniture but had established some credit and were able to furnish their new home at the Sears store in the largest city near them. Ann likes to tell the story of when they went to buy the furniture that Lee insisted on "negotiating" with the sales person. No one ever heard of much negotiation at Sears, but Lee managed to get more for their borrowed money than they had originally thought was possible.

The second year of Lee's career he and Ann were still struggling financially and were both away from their hometown. God blessed them by bringing a new young couple, Dave and Kathy, to the school where they were serving, and the four became instant friends. Both families had no money and were just surviving paycheck to paycheck. At the end of the pay period, the two couples would pool their money together and buy food to be prepared at one or the other's home. These were great times of bonding with new friends, and Lee and Ann have both told me that it brought them much closer together and caused them to depend heavily on each other.

Dave coached with Lee his second year. During Lee's first year of teaching and coaching he had developed a love for football, even though he had never played, by being around the team and getting to know the head football coach. The second year the head football coach asked Lee to share responsibilities with Dave to team coach the seventh and eighth grade football teams. Because Lee wanted to learn more about the game and ultimately coach the sport, he readily accepted the offer, realizing he would have to lean on Dave for all the knowledge of the game.

The first day of practice and the day to hand out the equipment for the players, a young seventh grader came up to Lee to ask him what a specific piece of equipment was. You see, the youngster had never played football before. Lee, in his most polite and face-saving method, coolly told the aspiring athlete he would have to ask Dave (who happened to be standing close by). When the young man turned to look at Dave, Lee also turned, thinking he was about to learn his very first lesson in the sport of football: what equipment was what. The look of alarm on Dave's face set waves of panic through Lee, and they reverberated back through Dave as well. It seems someone had forgotten to ask either of the young coaches if they had ever played or coached football. Both mistakenly thought the other had football experience, and both assumed they would just be helping and not really coaching.

Again, the Paul Harvey "rest of the story" is the best part. These two young, naïve, clueless coaches took on the task with vigor and enthusiasm and lost only one game the entire season on both the seventh and eighth grade teams. Of course, they had good young kids, but both Lee and Dave worked hard to educate themselves about the game and pass the knowledge on to their young charges. Much of their success was a direct result of being under a wonder man who was the head coach. Much like Lee's mentor in basketball, this football coach was the kind of man, father and coach Lee aspired to be.

In one of our later conversations, I asked Lee what made this man so distinctive:

Jim Bardwell was a very special man. I was very fortunate to have watched him as he coached, taught and raised his family during the first years of my career. What I saw in him was a man who cared. He cared about winning, but he cared more about the people he coached than the record he accomplished. He had the most unique way of relating to students and athletes. He expected much out of them, but he respected them as well. I never thought, as I am sure his players did, that football was more important than family or school. He was an excellent teacher and set high expectations from his students and never let them slack off in their classes. You could just tell Jim loved kids and loved what he did for a living.

I also remember how in practice he could be very intense and worked the athletes very hard. But often in the middle of practice someone would do something that other coaches would probably scream and yell about, and Jim would say something funny, and the entire team would laugh so hard the practice would for all purposes just stop. He would laugh with them, let them enjoy the laughter and just as quickly as it started it would stop, and they would go right back to the intensity they had before the laughter. I just marveled at how he could bring joy into a practice that others would fail to initiate. He was very successful as far as football was concerned, but he was more successful in making a difference in many young men and women by his caring and his example.

Here was yet another example of a man who influenced Lee and his walk through his professional and personal life. It was because of men like Jim Bardwell who took the time to trust, enable, empower and expect excellence out of Lee that helped him to be a better teacher, coach and father. Examples such as Jim also helped Lee to help others to better themselves as well.

Lee encountered others who were not helpful or good examples for him. In contrast to Jim, there were others who would have taken Lee in the wrong direction had he allowed it to happen. Even in the same school and on the same coaching staff there were people who were evidently out for no one but themselves and cared little about their students, athletes or their families. One such person even tried to use Lee's youth, lack of knowledge and good nature to promote himself. Luckily Lee realized what was happening before it was too late and distanced himself from the selfish individual. This person ultimately took advantage of his status as an educator to prey on a young girl and lost his career, family and self respect.

Joy and Sadness

During the second year of Lee's tenure at his first teaching position Lee and Ann's second son, Aaron, was born. It was a joyous occasion, and even though money was tight, the joy of their second son could not be damped. From early on Aaron seemed to have some health issues. He was sick more than Allen had ever been, and at one point early in his young life became very ill. He developed a strange rash, and doing all she knew how to do, Ann could not seem to clear up the baby's skin. The rash soon developed into sores that were mostly confined to the baby's diaper area. Of course the two young parents were scared and took the baby to the local hospital where he had been born. A young foreign doctor who spoke broken English roughly examined little Aaron, and in a very rude, quick manner looked at the anxious couple and said, "Wash baby!" He then turned and walked out of the examination room. The two were completely devastated. Lee shared with me that he had never been as angry at another human being as he was at the doctor. Ann was shaken and crying because she knew the care she had been giving the young baby. The doctor had not even taken the time to examine the inside of the baby's mouth where, too, there were some sorts of ulcers showing in his cheeks.

The distraught parents went home and tried to figure out what to do. The last option they felt they had was a somewhat disreputable doctor just across the street from their humble little rental in an old house. There were stories around the small town that the doctor was himself a drug addict, and few young families would even consider walking into his office. Lee and Ann were desperate, and desperate parents do desperate things to help their children. They reluctantly took Aaron across the street and the doctor saw him immediately. He carefully examined the child and took cultures from the inside of the baby's mouth. He then disappeared into an adjacent room, looked at the cultures under a crude microscope, and came back to announce he knew what was inflicting the child. It seems it was some sort of infection that was inside the baby, and each time he wet his diaper, the infection was spreading outside and causing the rash as well as the ulcers in the mouth. The old, washed up doctor had taken the time to listen, observe and examine the young child so he could successfully diagnose the problem and then successfully treat it. As a result, the baby was restored to health.

Lee and Ann learned a valuable lesson through this ordeal, a lesson we all need to learn: appearances and rumor do not tell the entire story. Yes, this old doctor was not polished in his appearance and did not have a fancy office; he just practiced medicine and took the time to heal those who came to him sick. The other part of this lesson is that he knew the young couple was struggling and had two small children, and his fees were embarrassingly low.

Would our world not be a better place if we had more who cared like the old doctor versus the young doctor who did not have the time to spend actually doing what he was supposed to do? Would we not be better people, husbands, wives, teachers, coaches, business men and women, pastors, or whatever God has chosen as our life's work, if we would take the time to listen, look, think and determine how we can help those in our sphere of influence?

26

The Next Move

LEE LEFT HIS FIRST JOB after just three short years. Lee had an opportunity to leave after the second year to go to a larger school in the northern part of the state, but when he went to finalize the contract it was not as it had been promised, so they stayed south for the third year. That same school corporation recruited him the next year, however, and Lee accepted the position. One of the main reasons for the move was that it would allow Lee to attend Purdue University to work toward his master's degree. He had taken some classes while south, but his desire was to go to Purdue. He also wanted to become a head basketball coach, and the larger school would help him reach that goal.

That move turned out to be a short stop. Lee and Ann rented a house in the country but were only there for one year. Lee and the coach he worked under had some good success (at least in comparison to the seasons before their coming), and that made Lee very attractive to some schools as a head basketball coach. It also didn't hurt that Lee taught English, and there were not many head basketball coaches at that time in the state who were trained English teachers.

Toward the end of the first and only year at the second school, Lee was offered a head basketball coaching position at a small school in the northwest quadrant of the state. He accepted, and once again the young family had to pick up and move while Lee continued to work toward his master's degree. All this was continuing to have a huge financial burden on the struggling family, but Ann's willingness to pack up all their belongings and begin another journey with him was unshakeable; she never questioned this decision.

With the raise in salary Lee got with the new position and, strangely enough, because he still didn't make much money, they were able to obtain a special government loan to buy a house in the new community. It was an older home, but well kept and on a beautiful tree lined street. On one of my visits to the home, I noted to Lee that they had come a long way, but his response was they still had a long way to go. You see, Lee had always set goals for himself and the aspiration of being a head basketball coach within five years of his graduation had come to fruition. He had reached his dream, but was already looking past that dream to his next of becoming a school administrator. Maybe his looking beyond the present was one of the reasons for Lee's failure as a head coach.

This young enthusiastic young man in one year became a defeated, unhappy person as a head coach. Lee, for the first time in his life, could not find any success in the basketball position. Even though he had never had great success before, he had always had some measure, but not so in this new position. Although Ann and he were very content in their first new home, Lee's work pressures diminished much of the joy in their lives. At the same time Lee was away many evenings each week working toward his next degree.

Lee did have success in the classroom, but it could not outweigh his depression and the pressure he put on himself to win basketball games. After one weekend that was particularly gruesome, Lee had an epiphany about himself and coaching. He called the next week, we met, and he made some life altering decisions:

You know we have had a tough year. I know you and I have talked and we both believe the kids have talent, but I just can't get it out of them. Last Friday night we played a pretty tough team and should have won the game. I went on a tirade of emotions and just blasted the kids for the loss. I was really out of control. I had tried everything else so I thought I would try being someone I am not.

You know what? It worked. The next night we played great and beat a team we shouldn't have even been close to. We had a kid set new school records for scoring and it looked like a totally different team. The problem was that I felt horrible, and I think the kids did too. I had managed to take the joy right out of the game for the kids and me too. The fans were happy, but I had done more to harm the relationship I had developed with those kids than I could ever hope to recover.

If I have to be someone I am not to get kids to win, I am not going to continue to do it. Winning isn't worth it. These kids deserve more than that, and I have let them down. I am going to finish my administration program and get into leadership as soon as I can. Hopefully I can

*help other coaches to see what is important and not make
the same mistakes I have made.*

Another issue that probably helped steer Lee to his career
change mentality was the tragic loss of one of his players. Lee
had a young man who was really not a very skilled player. He
was, however, a fine young man of high moral character and well
thought of by all his peers. He was a junior and was not going
to make the varsity team. Lee sat the young man down and explained where he was as a player and that he would not be making
the varsity team. The child was bright and knew his abilities, but
loved the game and pleaded with Lee to allow him to remain on
the team and play on the reserve team to try and hone his skills
so he could help the varsity members at a later date. Reluctantly,
Lee allowed the request.

Not long after the decision, the young athlete and his friend
had pleaded with their parents to let them go to a movie on a
Sunday night. Both sets of parents were wonderful, caring people
and after much discussion allowed the two to talk them into going out. As they were entering the small town where the theater
was located, the other boy who was driving turned into the path
of an oncoming vehicle and Lee's young player was killed. Lee
second guessed himself at such a level that he started to sink into
depression. Not until he met with the parents at the funeral home
and talked to the father was Lee able to cope with the death. He
found himself counseling the dad that it was not his fault that his
son had died, and this somehow helped Lee realize he had done
nothing to harm the child.

On a side note there was another story to be told about this
incident:

You know that I lost a player in an accident. His name was Gary. As a part of my class, Sports Literature, he had to broadcast a junior high basketball game, tape it, write the commercials, etc. Well, I don't know whether you knew it or not, but Gary's mother teaches with me. She came down to my room the other day and asked if I still had the tape with Gary's assignment on it. She took the time to tell me how much he had enjoyed the task and how proud he was of his work. She thought if she could have the tape she could have at least his voice to hear once in a while. I searched all my old tapes, listened for his and you will not believe what I found. Of course I have to reuse most all of the tapes and when I found the one Gary had used this is all that was left...

"This is Gary...good bye."

I couldn't tell his mother. I just could not give that to her with only those words left of her son. I kick myself over and over again for not keeping the tape, but I had erased it before he was killed

Although there were many reasons for Lee's quick departure from the head coaching ranks, this experience in losing one of his kids had a profound effect on him. He realized he was now in a position to help those who were more like him than he wanted to believe. He now carried a new burden in his heart—a burden to make sure he positively impacted children under his care.

27

Launching Into Leadership

NOTHER PERSON IN LEE'S LIFE who had a huge positive impact was Dr. Charles Carress, a professor at Purdue University. Lee went to Dr. Carress' office to talk about how to go about getting certified to be a principal. Once again, God blessed Lee with a man who took the time to listen and invest in Lee. Dr. Carress listened to Lee's goals and counseled him to get his principal license at the same time he was getting his master's degree. Few knew then and even now that this was possible. By getting this most valuable advice, Lee was able to speed up the plan to meet his goals, and at the end of the traumatic year as head coach, he finished his master's degree and became a licensed administrator.

As was and is characteristic of Lee, he let no time pass and actively began to seek administrative positions as soon as he found out he could be licensed within the year. It was not long before he started getting responses, and he quickly found a position as assistant principal and athletic director at a larger school in the suburbs of the capital city. There were many reasons why this was a good move: more money, no coaching, closer to both his and Ann's families. The negative, however, was that this was the third move in three years, and the financial strain on the young couple was overwhelming. True to form, however, Ann cheerfully packed up the house and the children and they went on to their next adventure.

This move brought new challenges. While at the former school system, Ann and Lee had decided they would try and have another child. They tried for several months and nothing happened, so they decided to sell their baby furniture and clothes and, because they were going to be moving again, they would just end their family with the two boys God had blessed them with. But God had other plans ... just before the move they found they were pregnant again. They quickly went back to the fellow teacher who had bought the baby furniture and asked if they could please have it back. The man had not paid for it yet, so reluctantly he agreed, and Ann and Lee packed up the truck and moved to the suburbs.

Lee made the move to his first administrative role only one short year after he had become the head basketball coach at the other school. Although Lee was quickly moving up in his profession, he was putting his family through much turmoil in making the frequent moves. It brought to mind Lee's early family life with the number of moves precipitated by his father. The difference was significant, however, because Lee was moving because his career was improving, yet his moves early in life were because the family was continuing to be in need.

Lee was very fortunate and blessed in his first leadership position to be serving with one of the best principals in the state. Lee could not have had a better mentor. Bob Kelso was from the "old school" of leadership on the surface. If someone didn't know him and his heart, they would have perceived him to be a dictatorial leader who ran his school with an iron fist. Once you knew Bob, however, you knew that his success as a leader had less to do with the perception and more to do with his heart. He had a genuine love for the children and staff he led, and he held high expectations for both. He was perceived as a tough leader, and he was, but he led with a sincere devotion to his profession and those he served.

Lee served as assistant principal and athletic director for a school of approximately 1200. He was the sole disciplinarian for the school while filling the role of athletic director. This combination made for a very stressful position that required much time away from his family. When talking to Lee about this position, he expressed that he learned more than he ever dreamed he could, but with the learning there was a toll to be paid in sacrifice of time away from his beloved family. It was even more demanding, as far as time was concerned, than serving as the head basketball coach in his previous position.

Lee learned a valuable lesson early in his career as leader that many never learn. He learned he had to find his own leadership style and not be a "mini" Bob Kelso or be someone that others expected him to be. Early as the "hatchet" man in discipline, Lee learned what he had to do to succeed:

I had a really tough first year as assistant principal. I started out thinking I had to be this stern, take-no-prisoners type of principal and felt the only way I could get the students to respect me was if they feared me. Wow, was I wrong. I really forgot quickly what I had learned all those years of my life and started out treating kids with little respect and tried to force them into proper behavior rather than lead-

ing them to it and modeling it myself.

One night Ann and I heard a disruption outside our house, and by the time I got my clothes on and got out to investigate, I had (believe it or not) 53 bags of garbage thrown into my front yard. It first made me angry and hurt that someone would do that to me. After much internal soul searching and honest self analysis, I realized I probably deserved every bag. What I am saying was that I was trying to demand respect from the students rather than earning it by the way I treated them. I was also very unhappy and realized it was because I was trying to be what I thought others wanted me to be rather than be who I really was. Once I began to be myself, the students and staff both responded to me much better, and we were able to significantly reduce discipline problems in the school by letting students know we had high expectations, but we also respected them. I learned that I needed to try and stop the unacceptable behavior, but also realized I needed to try and help (if I could) what was actually causing the behavior.

Isn't it true that, just like Lee, many of us try to take on personas we really aren't because it is what we think people expect from us? Many times, especially in leadership, if we would just be ourselves, be humble and learn what makes us operate at our maximum efficiency, we would be much more successful. Trying to be someone you aren't will make for a very unhappy and unproductive professional and personal life.

During the first year of Lee's career in school administration, the birth of their third and final son took place. This blessing came in the form of a 10 pound 6 ounce healthy baby boy. He didn't come easy as Ann was in labor for one full week before he finally decided it was time to come join the family in their small brick suburban home. Anthony came to the world to join his brothers Allen and Aaron to make the family complete.

Lee stayed in the assistant principal/athletic director position for three years and had a fulfilling life. They were able to improve the small home they purchased, and it became the first real home they had. Lee had many valuable experiences and was mentored carefully by Bob to prepare him to become a principal. As a matter of fact, at the conclusion of his second year as assistant, Lee was approached by a neighboring school and asked to become their principal. When Lee talked to Bob, it was decided another year of learning was needed. At first Lee was bothered by Bob's reaction, but he trusted him, and Bob assured Lee that he would help him find a position at the end of the third year. As was always the case, Bob was a man of his word, and at the conclusion of Lee's third year as assistant, Bob helped him find his first principal's position.

On a side note, shortly after Lee went on to his leadership role of a small junior/senior high school, Bob became terminally ill. Lee would often go back and visit his old friend, and they would talk on the phone and set "living goals" together. What this meant was they would mutually agree on things Bob wanted to live to see. For example, he desired to witness his daughter graduate from college and to see a troublesome person at central office retire. Bob finally lost his battle with cancer, but lived his life out at the end with a dignity and purpose few could match. Up until the week before he died, he was still at his desk serving the school and students he loved so much. He was in tremendous pain, but never let it affect his performance of his leadership duties.

Another Move, Another Degree

During Lee's tenure as assistant principal and athletic director he had continued his studies at Purdue and finally received his master's degree. As was the case, however, this was not the end for Lee, but the beginning of another educational journey as he began his work toward another degree, educational specialist, at Ball State University. In his tenacious workmanlike manner he took on the new principal position and pursued his next degree all at the same time. Again Ann wholeheartedly supported and helped to see that the goal could be achieved. If Lee could finish the degree, this would allow him to fulfill the next ambition he had established: to be a superintendent of schools. Here was a young man who, when I first met him, was not sure if he would ever succeed at anything, and now he was working on his third college degree and well on the path to being the leader of a school corporation.

Lee didn't even realize how quickly that dream would come true. He managed to finish his degree, and in December of his third year as principal he got his superintendent's license. At this time Lee was only 32 years old, and had no idea that anyone would be interested in his services as a district leader.

To his and many others' surprise, Lee was contacted by a small school corporation in the central part of the state and became a candidate for their top educational spot. Still, Lee, Ann and the leaders of the school he was serving didn't think there was any chance the school board would select someone so young and lacking central office experience. As had been the case many times before in Lee's short career, however, he interviewed and was offered the position. He and Ann prayed about it, and he accepted the position. Lee began his superintendent career in January and became at that time the youngest sitting superintendent in the state.

He stayed at the first superintendent position for four years and then left the small school for a much larger one. As a matter of fact, in his second school system he had as many students in the high school alone as he had in the entire corporation in his first. During this second position, Lee once again decided to go back to school and chase his dream of earning his doctorate. At the beginning of the quest it seemed daunting to the young family, but Lee and Ann persevered, and Lee went to school at nights and in the summer to complete his coursework. At the same time he began doing his research for his dissertation and, after six years of work, Lee now stands in front of me and my family as we sit in Elliot Hall of Music at Purdue University to watch this person we followed all these years be hooded and receive his Doctorate of Philosophy.

Lee culminates his educational journey not with a period but with an exclamation point as he is hooded for his doctorate degree.

28

The Truth Revealed

THIS IS WHERE THE STORY BEGAN, but this is not where this story ends. It is time as an author I give you the "rest of the story." You see, I have not been totally truthful with you, the reader, through this book. I hope you will forgive me. I have been truthful as to the content, but not the way it was written.

I am Dr. Al Long, the author, but I am also Lee.

This was not an easy story to tell. My family and others had encouraged me to tell my life story, but I didn't know how to do it—how to pull out and face the demons from my past and be able to objectively report them, while also trying to be positive about how great my life had become with the support of a loving family and many who have positively influenced me. It was a daunting task and one that, for me, was only possible by approaching the memories from a "third party objective" perspective.

Writing this book was and is the most difficult thing I have ever had to do. There are many stories not told that perhaps should be, and many that shouldn't be told that will go with me to my grave. Some things in my life were so painful that only God and I know about them, and that is the way it will stay.

My purpose began to change as did the title as I was penning the words. I experienced many revelations about "Lee" as I was writing these pages. At one point I was in a hotel on a business trip adding to his journey when it suddenly became evident to me why I feel and act the way I do many times in social situations. I know people perceive me as aloof, and I would probably have the same perception, but that is not the case. Today, even though I have achieved much success in life, have a wonderful family and in the world's eyes have attained the American dream, inside I am still the fat 12-year-old that you first met in Dr. Long's classroom. To be able to make it through some situations that occur routinely in my life, especially social events, I still many times fall back on my old tendency of being "alone in a crowd." It is the only way I learned to survive, and I still revert to those feelings and emotions deeply ingrained in me for so many years.

Drop the Rock!

I recently had a very close friend read an early manuscript of this book to see if it made any sense and if she could catch the vision cast in the pages for hope and joy of a life changed by people who care. She thought the book a bit dark, and she also told me that when she got to about page 100 in the typewritten document, she stopped and told her husband that if Lee didn't reconcile with his father she was going to be very angry. At that juncture I asked her if she was angry, and she said yes. In the early writing I really had no closure.

This fact had really bothered me, but I rationalized my lack of action based on the hurt and bad experiences I had as a young, overweight child. I just had never been able to get past my childhood wounds and had convinced myself that I was right and everyone who told me differently was wrong. I had counseled and encouraged others to "get over it" and reconcile with a loved one, but never saw that a necessity in my own life. It's like spinach to me; it seemed healthy and good for others, but not necessarily for me.

I continued in my denial until just recently. My mother, still vibrant, is getting older and since my dad had passed, had lived alone for many years. Her physical body, like all will someday do, is breaking down, so we talked and decided it was time to move her closer to family so she wouldn't be alone and we could check on her more often. It was during this time when the first event happened that pushed me to where I needed to be emotionally. When my sister Sue and her husband came to aid in the move, we had a chance to talk, and she read what I had written about her in Lee's story. It moved her to tears. As we hugged and cried, she told me that this was the first time in her life anyone had acknowledged what she had lived through. I am sure that a step in healing took place that day for my sister. Since then we are writing each other and calling as we can, and each conversation ends with "I love you" ... something I had wanted for a long time, but didn't do enough to ensure that it took place. Reconciliation number one!

The next day at church the second reconciliation opportunity came about. Isn't it wonderful how God works and how His plan comes to pass at times when we least expect it? Our church was to celebrate communion on this particular Sunday. Many denominations celebrate communion in different ways and at different times. Communion is taking the bread and wine in remembrance of the sacrifice of the body and blood of Christ. Our pastor, a longtime friend, always seems to come up with wonderful ways to make special times even more special. On this particular Sunday, as we entered the sanctuary, we each were given a small rock. There was no explanation—just the rock. As we entered to sit and begin the service, we noticed the communion tables up front as they many times are, but there were some additional items. In front of each communion table sat a metal bucket on a small stand.

Of course, knowing our pastor, Greg, no one had any idea what was going to take place. As he began to prepare us for the communion, he used scripture from 2 Corinthians, the story of the adulteress woman who was standing accused. The religious leaders known as Pharisees were goading Jesus and trying to disgrace him in public. As they accused the woman and questioned Jesus, he bent down and slowly began to write in the dirt. Many believe, as do I, he was writing the sins of the accusers in the dirt before them.

The penalty for adultery was stoning. The Pharisees and probably many others had stone in hand just waiting to pronounce retribution for the crime. When Jesus told those gathered that whoever was without sin should cast the first stone, one by one the people dropped their stones and withdrew. The accusers walked away from the one they had accused.

Pastor Greg then went on to drive home his point by stating that we were not much different from the people gathered there on that day—that many times we stand in judgment of others while we have sin in our own lives. He further stated that we, in this story, could be both the accused and the accusers. He instructed us that before we went forward to partake of the sacraments that we should examine ourselves and our relationships and assess whether or not we needed to "drop the rock" of judgment.

As I sat there, I began to pray and was totally convicted of my sin of not "dropping my rock" toward my dad. I had the visual image of my dad in the place of the woman and myself standing there with rock in hand ready to stone him for his past actions. I will admit I wept openly and asked God's forgiveness for my rock I had carried for so many years. As I went forward and dropped the stone that had been given to me at the beginning of the service, the sound echoed through the walls of the church and pierced the walls of my heart. It was as though the rock that had been in my heart for so long was finally gone.

I would love to tell you that I have not picked up another rock since that communion experience, but when I get those feelings and emotions welling up in me, I simply say to myself, "Drop the rock." I would encourage those of you who have read this book to do the same if you harbor resentment or bitterness you need to get rid of. I think many of us carry sacks of rocks around all the time, and they drag us down from being the kind of people God created us to be—free of emotional burdens and able to reach out in love to others like Lee.

I believe my life is a journey, and I am in a continual process of being healed and refined by my Creator. I know that I lived through these experiences so that I would gain compassion and empathy for others who deal with the same struggles, so that I might be able to someday help someone else. While I am in no way completely healed, I have found a new place of freedom, fulfillment and joy on the other side. One of my greatest joys now comes from teaching and speaking. I feel happy and energized when I am helping people and making a difference in their lives. As an educator it is a great honor and source of satisfaction to play a part in the process of preparing principals to lead. To know that I am having an impact on future leaders, guiding and teaching men and women how to lead, watching them grow and creating a positive and long lasting impact for future generations—it is these times when I am not focused on myself but on the interests of others that I feel most at peace, most alive.

But the true heart of my success, my crowning achievement, is knowing that the cycle of emotional poverty in my family has been broken. Ann and I designed our family in a purposeful way based on three covenants: 1) Christ is at the center of our family, 2) we will never disagree on discipline issues in front of our children, and 3) we will always sit together as a family at church. I believe that in keeping these oaths, my family and my children's families will not be like my own childhood. This is the legacy I leave to future generations.

I still have work to do on myself. That fierce fear of failure still lingers in me, driving me to achieve more, to do more, to stifle the feelings of low self esteem that still plague me. Yet as screwed up as I may be, I am most happy now when I am outside myself, thinking about others, doing things for others, giving my time, my money and my help…that is when my past eludes me for a brief time and I happily forget to be alone in a crowd.

Epilogue: What Can We Do?

IF YOU HAVE GOTTEN NOTHING from reading these words other than the fact that you can make a difference in a child's life, then the work and emotion it took to get this from my heart and mind down on paper has been worth the effort. As a person who has devoted my life to the profession of education, I passionately want people to understand how they can impact young lives. I still think to this day about those individuals who were such powerful, positive influences on me and, likewise, I think of those who did things that hurt me and ultimately my family.

If you are a father: Love and affirm your children. It is easy to criticize, judge, and rebuke your children, but don't forget to spend as much time or more building up as you do rebuking. Please don't get me wrong—you do need to discipline and have high expectations, but love your children unconditionally. I reflect back on my life and see how it could have been so much different if my father would have given me affirmation. The interesting thing is, after his death, I learned that he spoke positively about me many times to others, but he never took the time to tell me how he felt. Please don't make that same mistake. Take the time to celebrate and enjoy your children every step of their lives. It will not be easy at times, but it will pay huge dividends as they grow older.

If you are a mother: Love and discipline your children. Sometimes love means doing the hard thing. Your discipline may seem harsh to a child at the time, but oftentimes you will be protecting your children from potential harm that they may never understand. They do not see the long-term effects of their choices as you do. So even when it feels like you are taking something away from them or preventing them from having what they want, you can know that you are making decisions that ultimately are protecting and caring for them—and that is what love is all about.

If you are a teacher: Care about ALL of your students. I gave a seminar recently on raising student achievement and showed research that says students will achieve at a higher level if they have teachers who care. When sharing my three months of research, a young man casually said, "Isn't that just common sense?" The answer is yes, but isn't it tragic that many still don't do it? A lot of children who come through the doors of our schools and into our classrooms are not very loveable. For whatever reason, they don't look like, talk like, smell like, or behave like we think they should, and we therefore treat them differently or like they have no hope of achieving. I was one of these children—not a very easy one to care about. It would have been much easier for several of my teachers to just give up on me and let me fall through the cracks of life. Spend the time to know your students and invest yourself in seeing that they have a chance to make life a joyful journey. The research shows dramatically that children will most likely rise to the expectations you set for them or fall to the expectations if you set them too low. Treat each child as a gift and a surprise that is just waiting to be opened to new and better experiences.

If you are a student like Lee: Know that there is a way out of your circumstances. Don't accept the status quo and think that you have no chance in life. You can do as much as you want with your life with the talents God has given you. But don't believe you can be *anything* you want, either; that is a deception perpetuated by the world. Many get dejected and quit because they can't be something they are not gifted to be. The reality is that God has given you a talent; just find it and use it to make your life the very best it can be. Also allow and seek out others to help you. Don't make the same mistake I made most of my life by isolating yourself and feeling you have to do everything on your own. Often there are many people who are in your immediate sphere of influence who stand ready to help. You have to let them know you need help, and then you need to be ready to accept it. On the other hand, please don't abuse the aid offered by others. Avoid the mentality that you are entitled to certain privileges and that everyone should do for you no matter what the circumstances. You have to work hard and have a plan to be sure you succeed. It is really not everyone else who has to make you succeed and break the chain of failure; you have to be the main hammer and chisel. Those who come alongside of you may help, but you are responsible for your own destiny.

If you are a leader: Lead with love and compassion. It is easy to drive people with force and intimidation, but to guide lovingly is much more difficult. Lee was blessed to have people who showed him how to lead with love and compassion. Be a servant and shepherd and care for your sheep, those you are blessed to be leading. At the time of this writing, I teach at the university level and prepare leaders. I passionately try to get them to understand what a blessing, but also what a huge responsibility, leading is. It is a blessing because you have such a platform and opportunity to change not only lives, but also organizations, for the better; by doing so you can change a community far beyond the walls of your own organization. Also be a leader of integrity. Until we have leaders who lead by principles and are less worried about paychecks, we will not have the type of organizations and leaders we need.

I leave you with some final thoughts and a poem.

- Constantly examine yourself and how you treat others.

- How can you positively impact someone in your sphere of influence today?

- What will be your legacy in life? Whom will you help to break the chain of failure in their lives?

- Love unconditionally, live life to its fullest, and make a positive difference in someone's life.

LIFE'S ROAD

It is said that life's a journey
    One we all travel in different ways.
From all directions troubles come
    It seems most all our days.

The way some handle life
    Is different from the rest
Some win, some lose and lose and lose
    Even trying to do their best.

What we do as people
    To help both young and old
Takes time, effort and dedication
    To help all travel life's road.

Had it not been for people
    Who showed they cared for me
The chain of failure would still be strong
    Instead of broken and me set free.

So what have you done for those
    You travel with each day?
Have you paused to help, stopped your quest
    Or simply gone your way?

For each you help along life's road
    Whether old or young, girl or boy
You will be blessed beyond belief
    And your life will be filled with joy.
              —Dr. Al Long

Power Publishing
5641 West 73rd Street
Indianapolis, IN 46278
(317) 347-1051
www.powerpublishinginc.com

LaVergne, TN USA
02 August 2010
191745LV00002B/1/P